Murders

May 25, 1853

The agonizing symptoms had come on suddenly. A little more than an hour earlier, as Timothy Lanagan ate his late lunch and drank a tumbler of beer, he was feeling fine. Now the excruciating pain in his stomach was so severe his face had become devoid of color. His skin was not the gray or green often associated with illness; instead, his flesh was almost transparent. When the pain had suddenly intensified, Lanagan was in the butcher shop owned by Burr Lord. Lord found himself compelled to look upon his sick customer in the same way people look at an accident they pass along the road. Years later the expression of anguish on Lanagan's face was still burned into the butcher's mind.

When the attack came on, Lanagan was in an area referred to as central Troy. Like all of us, when we are sick, he felt the compulsion to get to the security of home. Seeking compassion, sympathy, and treatment, he strained to get back to his humble residence. Lanagan lived in an area referred to, at the time, as upper Troy. Lanagan and his family had moved into the neighborhood the previous fall, intent on opening a small grocery store, which was in the same simple structure as his home. It was only seven or eight blocks from the butcher's to his home, but, because of his suffering, it took Lanagan the better part of an hour to make the walk.

There was an eccentric lady who lived in the same neighborhood as Lanagan. Analyzing this lady, she appears unlike most of those whom we see as peculiar today. She was not unusual in her physical appearance. She dressed normally, a little better than anyone else in the neighborhood, but her clothes matched, and she did not wear outlandish colors. She did not speak much differently from the rest of community; she may have used better language, but her voice and accent were not noticeably odd, especially in her neighborhood, which was heavily populated with immigrants. She was not particularly old, a trait that puts off some people. Actually, she was fairly young; most people believed her to be in her late twenties, perhaps her early thirties. This lady's strangeness was limited exclusively to her behavior.

The eccentric lady went by the name of Henrietta Robinson. Even though no one had ever met her husband, the strange lady was

Curse of the Veiled Murderess

The Story of Henrietta Robinson

First Edition

Compiled and Written

By

Dr. Hollis A. Palmer

Deep Roots Publications
Saratoga Springs, N. Y.

Curse of the Veiled Murderess
The Story of Henrietta Robinson

Published by:

Deep Roots Publications
Post Office Box 114
Saratoga Springs, NY 12866

©2004
By Dr. Hollis A. Palmer

Library of Congress Number 2004092361

Printed in the United States of America

ISBN 0-9671713-6-9

**This book is dedicated to my students for
the past two years.**

Anna
Elizabeth
Ilana
Jacob
Josh
Justin
Lianna
Li-Or
Michael
Sarah

**Hopefully you have learned that all knowledge does
not have to be practical**.

Special Thanks to:

Sharon Mitchell
For her help as my editor- we have grown together.

And

Jim Russo
For his help in making one more book look so good.

known as "Mrs. Robinson." She lived in a comfortable little white cottage, the yard of which backed up to the east bank of the Hudson River. Her home was on River Street, across from Lanagan's store. While Lanagan was struggling to get home, Mrs. Robinson had crossed the street to purchase a quart of beer at his grocery.

It was a few minutes before 3:00 p.m. when Mrs. Robinson entered Lanagan's establishment. While she was in the grocery, Mrs. Robinson learned that a guest of the Lanagan's, Catherine Lubbee, was ill in the back room. Although no one knew it at the time, Catherine and Lanagan had begun showing similar symptoms at almost exactly the same time. In a neighborly way, Mrs. Robinson went from the store into the back room to check on Catherine. Due to the severity of her condition, Catherine had been placed on one of the beds in the family's portion of the building. Seeing Catherine in her weakened state, Mrs. Robinson asked, "How are you feeling?".

Catherine, who by this time had already become frail, had to struggle to give her answer. "I am very ill," she responded. Catherine went on to accuse her neighbor for her illness. "You put something in my drink didn't you?" At 1:00 that afternoon, Mrs. Lanagan had accepted an offer for a free lunch from the Lanagans. The lunch was simple, comprised of an egg and a potato that was peeled by Mrs. Lanagan. In exchange for the gesture of friendship, Mrs. Robinson had insisted that she buy her hosts beer from their own stock. The beer that was drawn by Mrs. Lanagan was just enough to fill two tumblers. One of the tumblers had been consumed by Catherine Lubbee, the other by Timothy Lanagan.

Mrs. Robinson answered Catherine's accusation saying, "I put nothing in the drink but what would do you good." Realizing she could not help, and understanding that she was not wanted, the strange lady then went back into the grocery to purchase the beer that had been the purpose of her sojourn to the store.

With her husband out of the building, Mrs. Lanagan was minding the store. In a small establishment like Lanagan's, the person who minded the store had chores that were all-inclusive. Mrs. Robinson went to the counter and asked that a quart measure of beer be drawn. This was long before liquids, including alcohol, were pre-bottled. Mrs. Lanagan refused the sale, believing that her

3

strange neighbor was already under the influence of alcohol and not needing any more. There was a male customer in the store at the time. Mrs. Robinson asked him if he might like a drink. In all probability, Mrs. Robinson was hoping that, if he were to accept her offer, she would also be treated to some of the beer. Without giving an explanation, the man refused the overture.

When Lanagan ultimately reached the door to his store, the tenor of the room changed immediately. It was a few minutes after 3:00 p.m., when he was finally inside his grocery store. His wife could see immediately that he was in agony. The symptoms she witnessed appeared to be the same as Catherine's. Both were complaining of extreme abdominal pain that went right into their esophagus. Both were also suffering from diarrhea. Lanagan was so sick that he was unable to get into the bedroom under his own power. A family friend, William Buckley, who happened to be in store at the time, had to virtually carry Lanagan into the back room.

Lanagan's wife held the door open while Buckley helped her husband from the grocery into the other room. Buckley laid Lanagan down on the family's sofa. There, among the humble furniture, lay the husband on the couch and Catherine Lubbee on a bed. The simple unpainted structure had only two rooms. The front room was the store, and the back room was where the six members of the Lanagan family resided.

It was obvious that Lanagan's condition was grave. In a voice that was barely audible, he turned to his wife and said, "Run for the doctor."; almost as an afterthought, he added, "I am done for." She passed the order on to Buckley, who left to seek medical assistance. One of the Lanagan children went in search of the remainder of the Lanagan clan, many of whom lived in the neighborhood.

In the initial commotion, Mrs. Robinson had trailed the group into the family's residence. When those who had been assigned errands were out of the building, Mrs. Lanagan turned to the strange lady and said, "What have you done? You have killed the father of my children!".

The strange lady never flinched at the accusation. She responded, "No." A pause followed and then she added, "I have done no such thing." Her tone was strong and demonstrated an air of arrogance. One might even have called her haughty.

Hopefully in an effort to provide some assistance, Mrs. Robinson started in the direction of the prostrate Lanagan. He put up his hands in the universal gesture meaning "stop" and said, "Go, woman, go."

Feeling in her heart that the strange woman was somehow responsible for the anguish exhibited by those she loved, Mrs. Lanagan could not bear to have Mrs. Robinson's presence in the building any longer. She placed her hand against Mrs. Robinson's chest and said to her, "Go away." The strange lady resisted just enough not to be dissuaded from her purpose of remaining in the room. At that exact moment, Lanagan's mother, who was responding to the appeal of one of her grandchildren, entered the family's chamber. Lanagan's mother aided his wife in physically assisting Mrs. Robinson from the grocery.

Reluctantly, Mrs. Robinson had left the building, but her thoughts were still inside. She had a combination handyman, gardener who resided with her. He was known in the area as "Old-Man-Haley". The three words were all run together making his name sound like a four-syllable word. At Mrs. Robinson's request, Haley went to the store a short time later with a message requesting that Lanagan's wife come over to Mrs. Robinson's cottage. Mrs. Lanagan looked at Old-Man-Haley with an expression of utter confusion, then refused the request.

It was 3:30 by the time Dr. Adams, the Lanagan's family physician, arrived. Anna Lanagan, Timothy's wife, and his mother both told the doctor what they believed to have occurred. It should be noted that, as the incident continued to develop that day, Mrs. Lanagan continued to tell each of the people who would arrive on the scene what she believed to have happened. The mere fact that she was the first to tell the tale made her impressions the basis for everyone else's conclusions. There is one very important account that is missing. There is not a record of the conversations that must have transpired between Anna Lanagan and Catherine Lubbee before Timothy Lanagan got back from the butcher's.

Dr. Adams took one look at Lanagan and suspected, based on the symptoms Lanagan exhibited and from the conversations Adams had with the family, that Lanagan had been poisoned. Dr. Adams would later tell how the statements of the Lanagan family contributed to his belief that Tim Lanagan had been poisoned. His conclusion and treatment were not based exclusively on the symptoms exhibited.

After Mrs. Robinson left, and before Dr. Adams arrived, the Lanagan family had moved Catherine Lubbee to the home of Lanagan's cousin, James. James Lanagan lived in the same neighborhood, a couple of blocks south of Timothy's home. The relocation appears to be illogical. The Lanagan's knew that medical help was on the way. Although it might not be easy to treat two patients at the same time, no one had sent for a second doctor to help Catherine. The question of why a person, who was obviously in agony, was moved two blocks away from medical help was never asked or answered.

Lanagan was vomiting, had abdominal cramps and severe evacuations. Dr. Adams tried a variety of treatments to aid his patient. In an effort to dilute the suspected poison, Dr. Adams encouraged Lanagan to take water. In an effort to provide some relief, Dr. Adams administered pain relievers. Despite the medications administered by the doctor, the horrible retching would not stop.

Dr. Adams had a holistic theory of medicine. To Adams, a patient's attitude contributed greatly to his ability to overcome any illness. Shortly after Dr. Adams arrived, Lanagan told Adams that he sure he would not recover. Dr. Adams did not want Lanagan to give up. Based on his belief in the strength of the human spirit, Dr. Adams told Lanagan repeatedly that he might well recuperate. The doctor made his statement of assurance repeatedly, more to comfort Lanagan, than out of a sincere belief that it was the truth.

Until this cold rainy May day, Lanagan had been a vigorous man. Even in his current pain, he was able to lift himself from the bed when necessary. Lanagan knew that, despite Adams's encouragement, there was little chance of recovery. Lanagan kept telling the doctor that he was sure the outcome would be fatal. At one point, when Lanagan and the doctor were alone, Lanagan said of the cause of his condition, "A villain has destroyed me." He did not name the villain or even indicate the gender.

For a brief time, around 5:00 p.m., Lanagan appeared to be making a recovery. The retching did not stop, but he seemed to be stronger and in less pain. During this period when he was feeling better, Lanagan gave a statement as to what he thought had happened to him. Some would maintain that this was Lanagan's deathbed statement. The problem was that a deathbed statement had legal requirements. It could only be used in criminal court if the person who gave it did so with the full knowledge that he was dying. Dr. Adam's continued reassurances, even though they were not sincere, had eliminated this contingency legally.

As time slipped by, Dr. Adams became increasingly aware that he was in a serious situation. He felt it would be in his best interest, and that of his patient, to have the opinion of a second doctor. To provide assistance, or at least validation, Dr. A. J. Skilton, another doctor from the neighborhood, was summoned. Dr. Skilton arrived at the Lanagan's at about 5:00 p.m.. Skilton and Adams discussed the symptoms and their probable causes. They concurred that the reactions were the result of some mineral poison.

Mineral poison would indicate that the person had either taken the poison intentionally or had been given the poison by another person. In the case of plant poisons, a person could ingest them by accident (i.e. mushrooms). It is possible for a person to ingest a mineral poison by accident through substances including beer, apples and even water, but it is far more common for mineral poison to be deliberately ingested.

There was disagreement about the presence of a priest at Lanagan's bedside. Mrs. Lanagan, and only Mrs. Lanagan, said that there was a French priest at the house as her husband's condition deteriorated. When asked about the priest later, she could not remember his name. She was certain, however, that he no longer lived in Troy. The most that the others present could say to support her assertion is that there were many persons present.

About 6:00, Lanagan's condition became much worse. He lost most of his strength; his voice became frail. Finally and mercifully, Lanagan went into a coma. At approximately 6:30 that evening, in the company of his family, Timothy Lanagan's pain ended. Despite his initial diagnosis that all was lost, Dr. Adams claimed that he remained at Lanagan's side from the moment he arrived, over three hours before, until the moment of Lanagan's death.

Dr. Skilton knew that an autopsy would be needed to be sure

7

of the cause of death; he told the family of the requirement. The coroner, Dr. Reed Bontecou, came by later that night. Bontecou performed the autopsy the next morning in the Lanagan's home.

Early in the evening of May 25, Catherine Lubbee was informed of what had happened to Timothy Lanagan. Her doctors told her that, in all probability, she would not live. She provided a deathbed statement that would be accepted into evidence at the inquest that would follow. Her official statement was a series of responses to questions that were asked of her by the coroner, Dr. Reed Bontecou. For this reason, the statement appears somewhat jumpy. Her statement was:

I, Catherine Lubbee, have been duly sworn. I live in the city of Albany. I came to this city two weeks ago this Friday coming. I have been spending a part of my time with Mrs. Lanagan. I was at the Lanagan's store today about 1:00. I was well upon going there. Mrs. Robinson came in and ordered a glass of beer and some sugar for Mrs. Lanagan, herself and me. *Mrs. Robinson put about half the sugar in the beer.* I saw her put nothing in the sugar or beer except the sugar. She stirred it up with a spoon and asked me to drink one and Mrs. Lanagan the other. Mrs. Lanagan refused. Mrs. Robinson then asked Mr. Lanagan to take it. He came in from the grocery and drank the beer. She (Mrs. Robinson) pressed him to take it. I saw some white substance floating on the beer. Mrs. Lanagan attempted to remove the floating film off my beer. Mrs. Robinson told her 'no' that that was the best of it.

I never had any words with Mrs. Robinson, nor do I know of any cause of enmity; Mrs. Lanagan gave no reason for refusing to drink the beer other than she preferred it without sugar. Mrs. Robinson handed the drink to Mr. Lanagan to drink. I never heard that Mrs. Robinson hated Mr. or Mrs. Lanagan. Mrs. Robinson would have had ample opportunity to mix anything into the sugar, for full a quarter of an hour intervened between the time the beer was drawn and drank. Mrs. Robinson took the sugar and went into the store with it and then returned. Mrs. Robinson drank no beer, but even refused when I asked her to take some. I did not see any paper in Mrs. Robinson's hand. [This comment is in reference to an assertion made by Mrs. Lanagan that she had seen Mrs. Robinson put away a small piece of white paper.] The beer sickened me right off. At first I refused to finish the beer but was pressed by Mrs. Robinson. I was urged to take the sugar that was in the film. Mrs. Robinson took a spoon and took the dregs of the tumbler and forced it into the mouth of the witness. At that time I was already feeling sick, and I said to Mrs. Robinson, "it turns my stomach." Mrs. Robinson said to me, "You must take it for it will do you good." Mrs. Robinson told me that what she gave me and Mr. Lanagan in the beer was to revive our spirits. In the afternoon I asked Mr. Lanagan if he felt sick since drinking the beer.

There are several points that are raised in this statement that will be addressed later. The italics were added by the author.

**

Even before Lanagan died, the police were notified that there was a suspected poisoning. Based on the fact that they immediately were in search of Mrs. Robinson, it must be assumed that the complaint was filed by Anna Lanagan or her representative. Officer Charles Burns was on patrol in the center of the city when he received the word to be on the lookout for Mrs. Robinson.

At some point after Old-Man-Haley informed Mrs. Robinson that Mrs. Lanagan would not come over to discuss the situation, Mrs. Robinson decided to walk downtown. She either knew or assumed that she was suspected in the poisoning and that a complaint was to be filed with the police. At approximately 6:00 p.m., Mrs. Robinson stopped in Clark's Drug Store, on the corner of River and Federal Streets. This was the same store where she had purchased arsenic a couple of weeks before. She conversed for a few minutes with William Ostrom, the apothecary, who was sure of the time because he had just returned from tea. As on the previous Saturday, her face was flushed, and she seemed extremely anxious.

Mrs. Robinson acted out her nervousness by pacing around the store. She was unable to stand in one place for very long even as she conversed with Ostrom. When she spoke, her anxiety was apparent in her voice. Her personal appearance was very much out of character. Ostrom had known Mrs. Robinson for some time and thought of her as an "accomplished lady." This evening her dress was "in disorder and her language was bold." The only other time that Ostrom had seen Mrs. Robinson seem less than "accomplished" was on the previous Saturday evening when she had come to his store about 10:00 p.m.. On that Saturday night she seemed very stressed, possibly even drunk.

As she was pacing, Mrs. Robinson told Ostrom that she was being charged in an attempted double murder naming only Lanagan as a victim. Being naturally curious, Ostrom asked her what possible motive they thought she would have for poisoning Lanagan. She said that it was because she had refused to loan the people $100. Ostrom thought it strange that she would be suspected of killing for refusing to grant a loan. It is much more common for people to be upset, to the level of seeking revenge, for being refused a loan. Ostrom did ask why she would not give the Lanagan's money, if they needed it. Mrs. Robinson said it was because she did not want to draw that much cash from the bank in the absence of her husband.

She went on to tell Ostrom that she was in fear of her neighborhood. He advised her to go to the police for protection. Without making any purchases, Mrs. Robinson left Ostrom's and headed down the street.

In due course, Mrs. Robinson left Clark's and went next door to the cabinet shop. Cabinets are one of the most difficult pieces of furniture to fabricate, so skilled carpenters would call their shops "cabinet shops" when in fact they would make any piece of furniture. Mrs. Robinson was inside considering the purchase of a new bed frame when she was approached by Officer Charles Burns of the Troy Police. Burns had been given her description and went up to Mrs. Robinson and simply said, "Good day."

"Are you a police officer?" Mrs. Robinson asked.

Burns assured her that he was and took her into custody. This arrest had to be one of the more bizarre in the history of Troy.

10

It was only a few blocks to the jail, so Burns elected to walk there with Mrs. Robinson. The two of them walked casually back to the station. As they walked, Mrs. Robinson seemed lighthearted, and her gestures were very animated, which Burns thought was abnormal for a prisoner. She apologized for her appearance, remarking how her dress was showing the effects of a rainy day. What Mrs. Robinson did not know was that at this time nearly all women who were arrested were charged with either public intoxication or with being a harlot, so by comparison she presented a well-dressed prisoner. Along the way, Mrs. Robinson asked if they were going to the city's Recorder's office. It would be revealed that Mrs. Robinson knew the recorder and had been in his office. Burns assumed that Mrs. Robinson thought that the arrest would need to be recorded before she would be placed in custody. Perhaps to avoid any conflict, Burns told her that they were on their way to the Recorder's. Mrs. Robinson failed to note that they were headed in exactly the opposite direction from the Recorder's Office.

As they approached the city jail, Burns indicated the building that was their goal. There were a group of men gathered on the corner opposite the jail. The men were conversing and joking, but did not appear to pose a threat. Mrs. Robinson asked Burns if she might walk up the side street alone while he waited for her on the steps. Although she never explained the reason for her request, Burns assumed that Mrs. Robinson did not want to be seen being taken into the jail by an officer. In what has to be one of the more bizarre aspects in the history of arrest of a person suspected of attempted murder, Burns allowed her to walk up the street, alone, for approximately half a block. She was never out of Burn's line of sight, and he watched her the entire time. When she reached the first brownstone, Mrs. Robinson turned around and walked back to the jail. Burns did not see her dispose of anything; the walk appeared to be more of an effort to gain her composure.

Mrs. Robinson seemed shocked as she walked through the doors into the jail. Burns thought her reaction was to the actually, structure of the edifice; however, it is equally possible that she thought she was going to be in the Recorder's Office. Inside the jail, Burns was met by Sheriff John Price and officer Nathan Camp. All three men were present when Mrs. Robinson underwent a preliminary search.

She was not forthcoming about the two pistols that were hidden in the bodice of her dress. In the words of the officers, the guns were "taken" from her. Barnes took some time to examine the guns. One of the guns was old and, if it were working, would only fire a single shot before it needed to be reloaded. Upon further examination, Burns decided that the singe shot gun was not even loaded. The other pistol was fairly new and had multiple barrels. It was Burns's opinion that, despite the fact that two of the barrels were loaded, neither would have fired because of rust on the hammer. (Although there were some cartridges at this time, most guns were still loaded through the barrel; that meant that the early pistols had to have a different barrel for each shot.)

It was going to be a busy evening for the county coroner, Dr. Reed Bontecou. As news of the poisonings reached the jail, Sheriff John Price sent for the coroner. Among other things, Price needed Bontecou to go to upper Troy to begin an investigation. Since the crime seemed to be centered at Lanagan's store, Bontecou went there first. From there he went to check on Catherine Lubbee at the home of James Lanagan. Eventually, he came to the jail to search Mrs. Robinson. Finally, he would return to Mrs. Robinson's

Rensselaer County Jail

12

home to search for evidence.

By the time Bontecou arrived at the store, Lanagan was already dead. Bontecou began a coroner's inquest into the cause of death. This was in the time before photography, so the coroner's inquest was started very quickly. Literally, the coroner would select twelve men who were citizens, and owned property (Yes. It was required that they be men) and who were readily available. They would examine the evidence right at the site. During the inquest, Bontecou learned that Catherine Lubbee was failing fast. Realizing that he could lose a witness, Bontecou went to James Lanagan's home to find out what information Catherine could provide relative to his investigation into Lanagan's death. As soon as he looked at Catherine, Bontecou could see that she was worsening rapidly. It was because he felt that her death was imminent that Bontecou wanted to get a statement. He was the person who recorded the statement that was previously offered.

It was odd that Bontecou, a physician, began the investigation into Lanagan's death before examining Catherine. Was he not told that this was a suspected double poisoning? Was he not told of her condition immediately upon reaching Lanagan's? If not, why had no one told him? If he was aware, why did he wait?

After Bontecou took Catherine's statement, he went back to the jail. In addition to the inquiry into Lanagan's death, Dr. Bontecou was called in initially to search Mrs. Robinson's person. There were no female guards or deputies, so the only person who could touch a woman was a doctor. When Bontecou entered the room where Mrs. Robinson was at first held, there were three other men present. They were the arresting officer Burns, Nathan Camp and Francis Brown. When Bontecou told Mrs. Robinson of his purpose, she offered no resistance, but rather stood and raised her arms to facilitate his efforts. Bontecou was struck by her presence that evening. Her eyes had a wild quality. Her conversation was absurd, and she did not answer any of the questions he asked.

At age 30, Bontecou had been a physician for nine years. The choice of a doctor who was relatively young would be questioned later in several different contexts.

Finding no weapons (the pistols having already been taken) or evidence of something that might cause injury, Bontecou told

Mrs. Robinson that he wanted her keys so that he might search her house. Why the coroner would be called upon to conduct the search is not clear; nor is it clear why, in a case of this magnitude, they would not have obtained a search warrant before going to the house. Bontecou was able to obtain her keys, but he could not remember later whether she had given them to him or if he had found them in her purse during his search for contraband. As Bontecou was leaving her cell, he asked Mrs. Robinson if there was anything she desired from her house. In one of her few coherent answers that evening, she acknowledged that she would like some clean clothes. Bontecou told her that he would bring some back before morning. Officer Barnes, who was not responsible for searching Mrs. Robinson's person, claimed later that he found a piece of white paper in one of her pockets. Finding nothing either in the paper or written on it, he threw the paper away. (Paper was often used as a container; that is why the issue of this particular paper not having contents is mentioned.)

Sheriff Price sent three men with Dr. Bontecou to search Mrs. Robinson's home. Although he was not a police officer, Bontecou was considered to be in charge of the search. When they got to her house, they found both more than they had expected and less. On the down side, there was no one at the cottage. Both the maid and Old-Man-Haley were gone. On the up side, it turned out that the small cottage was elegantly decorated. There was also a large supply of new household items, some still in their boxes. The four men searched the house from the garret to the basement. When they tried to lift the carpet in the bedroom, the men realized that it was tacked down. They pulled it up and found a man's watch, a locket, and a small piece of white paper clearly marked "poison". It would later be determined that the packet marked poison contained 60 grains of arsenic. There was a second wrapped paper. They took it into custody and later found that it contained Spanish Fly.

Having heard Lubbee's story that she believed the source of the poison was the sugar that had been placed in her beer by Mrs. Lanagan, Bontecou thought it wise to take the sugar from Lanagan's store for chemical examination. A truly brave man, Bontecou drank some of the beer to see if it contained arsenic. Several members of the coroner's jury also bravely volunteered to test the beer for arsenic. None of them became ill from the beer. At least none of them exhibited signs of poisoning; they may have experienced a slight hangover.

Before the long evening was over. Bontecou obtained a set of clothes for Mrs. Robinson. He took the clothes back to the jail before going home for the night. On his return trip to the jail, Bontecou did not see Mrs. Robinson.

***

The Troy Press reported the next day that "a large quantity of stolen goods was found at her residence – consisting of boots and shoes, jewelry, silverware," with an estimated value of $1,000. To further attack her character, the newspaper went on to say that the possession of those items were a "showing that this strumpet has kept a rendezvous for blacklegs and robbers of the worst character." It would later be learned that all these items belonged to Mrs. Robinson. The article does show that the press was predisposed to finding her guilty.

From the very first reports, the newspapers attacked Mrs. Robinson's character. They called her everything from a "public woman," to a woman "of disrepute." They also told their readers that the name Henrietta Robinson was an alias. Knowing that a woman in town who was using an alias and living off the fortunes of either criminals (*The Press*) or men in general (*The Times*) had been charged for the murder of two people challenged the infrastructure of even the refined rumor mill of Troy. Obviously, not knowing who she really was made it even more interesting and seemingly important for the city's gossips to claim to have established her identity.

The Times made an assertion that would support many of Mrs. Robinson's claims. They said that "attempts of late had been made to drive her from the neighborhood."

***

The day after Lanagan died, Bontecou was back at the Lanagan's where he performed autopsies on both Lanagan and Catherine Lubbee in the room where the family ate and slept. There were several doctors present during the autopsies, including Dr. Skilton. The stomach of each victim was removed and sent to Professor Daikin's for a chemical analysis. To the trained medical eyes of the physicians present, each stomach had the appearance of being subjected to poison. At the upper end of Lanagan's intestine, there was visible what turned out to be approximately 40 grains of arsenic.

The finding of the coroner's jury was printed in the *Press,* "the deceased, Timothy Lanagan and Catherine Lubbee came to their deaths by the effects of poison administered to them by Mrs. Robinson, with the premeditated intention of causing their deaths."

Arsenic

Arsenic is found in two forms. One is soluble; the second is not. The soluble form would have dissolved in the beer. Once in solution, arsenic is odorless, colorless and tasteless. Therefore, neither Timothy Lanagan nor Catherine Lubbee would have detected the element as they drank the beer. The problem is that in soluble form there would not have been any grains left floating in the foam. So where did the grains come from that were found in Lanagan's intestines? To have grains left after being put in the beer and passing through the stomach, the arsenic must have been ingested in the non-soluble form. This presents a different problem. Arsenic is heavier than beer and would have sunk to the bottom of the glass. In its non-soluble form, arsenic would not have been visible in the foam as Catherine had suggested.

Mrs. Lanagan and Catherine would both say that Mrs. Robinson had insisted they not skim off the foam, but the arsenic would not have been in the foam; it would have been in the bottom of the glass. Since Catherine did not finish her beer, she would not have gotten much, if any, of the non-soluble arsenic. Even the heartiest of drinkers would hesitate to drink the residue that formed in the bottom of some of the old beers. That raises the question of how Catherine Lubbee and Timothy Lanagan ingested the arsenic. Arsenic is a white tasteless powder that would have blended in perfectly with the potato. The two who were poisoned had eaten their potatoes before Mrs. Robinson arrived. Could it be that Mrs. Lanagan pealed their potatoes as she would admit to doing for Mrs. Robinson?

The Antecedents

Having aspirations beyond working all the daylight hours in a mill, in October 1852, Timothy Lanagan, his Anna and four children moved to a building on the corner of Vanderhayden and River Street where he opened a small grocery store. Until the time he opened the store Lanagan had worked as a butt-maker for several years; butt-maker was a metal worker who made hinges, and carriage springs. During this period in America, an immigrant from Ireland, such as Lanagan, occupied one of the lowest rungs of the social ladder; as a result, he had to take whatever position was available to him.

The building occupied by the family faced River Street, the more commercial of the two streets. The family converted the front room into a neighborhood grocery store. The six members of the Lanagan family, Timothy, his wife Anna, their three sons and one daughter all lived in the one remaining room.

The city of Troy was in the midst of a rapid, industrial-driven, expansion. Lanagan's store, in upper Troy, was located in the center of what had become the home to many of the Irish immigrants. Lanagan's operation was more than just a grocery; it became a local hangout. He sold beer and provided a place for some of the other men from his native Ireland to congregate. The men would buy beer, play cards and dawdle for hours.

In the mid-nineteenth century, merchants were trying to make a living, not a fortune. There were no franchises or massive super markets; mass transit was in its infancy, so people shopped in stores within walking distance of their homes. The neighborhood grocery store became a gathering place. Neighborhood merchants knew their customers intimately. Customers all used credit, paying the merchant whenever they were "called" or when they were paid for a day's labor. Merchants knew who they could trust to make good on an account, and they knew whose credit line they would not allow to get too high. This was the epitome of personalized America.

In the Victorian Era, roles within the family, regardless of social status, were well defined. If a family was of the labor class, the woman was the family manager, which meant that she shopped daily. Without refrigeration available to her, she picked up only what the family would use that day. Families did not stockpile; and, above all else, the woman was responsible for avoiding waste. On a typical day the "woman" would visit some combination of the grocery store, butcher shop and bakery. On occasion, usually weekly, the lady of the house would stop at the dry goods store. Similarly, men would stop at the newsstand on their way to work and at the tavern to enjoy a frosted mug on their way home. Every other Saturday morning, men went to the barbershop to catch up on politics and gossip. Children played in the streets until dark. Young couples sat on the stoop at night under the watchful eyes of older members of the clan. Families had a schedule; life had a pattern, and communities had a rhythm.

At the time of her death, Catherine Lubbee was only 25 years of age. She had never married, but had enjoyed a good reputation. Her sister was married to Anna Lanagan's brother. Unfortunately, Catherine's sister had passed away the previous fall as the result of a prolonged medical condition. Catherine had no direct family relationship to the Lanagans. The relationship between the Lanagans and Catherine Lubbee was based exclusively on the fact that Catherine's sister was Mrs. Lanagan's sister-in-law, and both families were Irish immigrants. During the time of Catherine's sister's confinement, Catherine had resided with the Lanagans. Because the illness was so long, Catherine had been forced to live with the Lanagans for about thirteen weeks during the previous autumn.

After her sister died, Catherine moved to Albany, where she took a position as a domestic. As the warm days of spring arrived, Catherine found herself out of work. Rather than paying for board, she elected to go back to Troy for a prolonged visit. She spent her days with Timothy and Anna Lanagan and slept each night at the home of James Lanagan, Timothy's cousin. Apparently James had better accommodations than the six-to-a-room that Timothy's family were used to. Catherine had stayed at the Lanagan's for a week and a half prior to her death. It should be noted for those not familiar with the area that Troy and Albany are fewer than six miles apart. Catherine could easily have taken the trolley home to Albany each night, if she chose.

There are some facts that should be kept in mind when examining the circumstances in this double murder:

- At 37 years of age, Timothy Lanagan took great pride in being a virile man.
- His heavyset wife was several years his senior.
- The couple had four children, all of whom should have been in school on the days that Catherine visited.
- Timothy Lanagan had helped his sister-in-law during her time of need the previous autumn. How far his support had gone and how grateful Catherine had been was the cause of speculation among some of the neighbors even before their deaths.
- With the exception of Mrs. Robinson, Mrs. Anna Lanagan was the only person left to tell the story of what had happened in the store that day.
- Mrs. Lanagan was in the store the entire afternoon of the murders and told each person, as he/she entered, her perception of what had occurred.

There is an expression that the first story we hear is the one we believe. Mrs. Lanagan was the first to talk with everyone.

Before the Lanagans' opened their grocery store, Mrs. Robinson traded at Peter Cox's store, a block further south on River Street at the corner of Vanderhayden. Mrs. Robinson's change of markets brought together a set of personalities that would impact on each other dramatically. Although Mrs. Robinson traded at the Lanagan's for six months, there was an upheaval, in the neighborhood, that came just before the double murder. The disturbance existed for less than half that period.

Like everyone else, Mrs. Lanagan used credit when she shopped at Lanagan's store. She always paid her bills in a timely fashion, using cash. Her bill at Lanagan's had, at one point, reached almost $14, which was paid cheerfully when she was asked to pay. On several occasions, she had also borrowed cash from the Lanagans always returning the money the next business day. Although the source of Mrs. Robinson's funds was not evident, her credit was excellent.

Mrs. Henrietta Robinson had moved from Albany to River

Street in Troy in early spring of 1852. This was approximately six months before the Lanagans moved to their store on the same street, and a full year before the murders. She lived in a modest, yet stylish, cottage, the back yard of which bordered the Hudson River. Her house stood well back from the road just north of the much grander home of the wealthy Oliver Boutwell. The Boutwell home obstructed the view of Mrs. Robinson's cottage, a fact that served her well. Boutwell was a successful businessman, owning several businesses including a grain mill. Boutwell's mill was also on the river just a little north of Mrs. Robinson's home. The grain for the mill was stored in silos which served as a magnet for rats and other rodents. To a lady like Mrs. Robinson, the presence of these vermin in the vicinity of her home was totally unacceptable.

Boutwell's Mill

From the very beginning of her residency in Troy, there had been considerable speculation about Mrs. Robinson's background. Having both a maid and a gardener, she lived well, but not lavishly or ostentatiously. She was polite to her neighbors but did not get involved in their dealings. When she first moved in, she rarely went out during the day. She was truly living a secretive life. Her seclusion added to her allure and mystery. Curiosity being a part of human nature, many of the neighbors were set on finding out her background. The very fact that this reasonably beautiful woman kept to herself caused speculation, rumors, and gossip to focus on her. It was understood by some of the neighbors that she was born in Europe. Some in the neighborhood thought that she was French; others were equally sure that she was English. There was even some supposition that she had attended Mrs. Emma Willard's Seminary; then, as now, this was a highly-esteemed institution. The two things that everyone could agree on was that she had refined manners combined with the ability to speak excellent French.

***

Readers should understand that the true identity of Mrs. Henrietta Robinson was never established during her lifetime. For the entire 52 years that members of the press would follow this story, the question of Mrs. Robinson's true identity would be constantly explored. Over the years she would frequently be asked about her background. With the possible exception of two incidents while she was in jail, her responses were never direct and always raised the level of interest even higher. In 1855, another author, David Wilson, spent considerable time researching Mrs. Robinson's background. He provided a name for this mysterious figure. This book will examine his findings and include updated information. This will be done in the same sequence as the story broke in the 1850's.

To add to the mystery, none of the neighbors ever saw or spoke to Mr. Robinson. Even more intriguing was the fact that Mrs. Robinson never received a letter from her husband. When she did speak of him, and that was only on rare occasions, she said that he was out "upon the rails." This was a term referring to the building of the railroads. At this early period in the Victorian Era, the railroads were like the Technology Revolution in the 1990's. Great fortunes were made and lost in just a matter of months. The implication of her characterization was clear; her husband was out making a fortune for them to share.

Mrs. Robinson never worked, yet she had a live-in gardener and, until just a few months before the double murder, a live-in maid. The source of her funds, like everything else about this woman, was a mystery to her little community. It was highly speculated that there existed family money on which she was able to live. This rumor was matched to that of her European birth. It was usually noted with a wink that it was far more likely that she was being "kept" by the mysterious man whose carriage would arrive after dark and leave before daylight. He was either not recognized by the neighbors or, more likely, they knew better than to use his name in open conversation. This man, if the neighborhood rumor mill was correct, was one of the most powerful men in New York State.

For over a year (spring of 1852 until spring of 1853), all had gone fairly well for Mrs. Robinson and her neighbors. She kept to herself, and they speculated about her. It was a symbiotic relationship, which in some bizarre way served both parties. Publicly, the neighbors left her alone, and she did not mix with them any more than was required to live. Privately, the neighbors were fixated on this mysterious woman. Without ever expressing it directly, she seemed to relish the mystery that she was creating.

It was in March of 1853 that the relationships and social structure of this little neighborhood began to unravel. Not until a full year after the murders would the reasons for these changes in associations and behaviors finally be explained. Not until this book would the full impact of the catalyst for the events that were to follow finally be grasped and explained.

As spring started to open its warm arms in March of 1853, Mrs. Robinson suddenly became an active member of the community. Until that month, she had always kept almost totally to herself. Suddenly, and without explanation, she came out of her cottage and into the social structure of the neighborhood. The transition was not at the invitation of her neighbors, but rather was motivated by changes in her own life. Suddenly, she began to seek out the company of some of her neighbors. It was as if she needed them to fill some void that had been created in her own life. On the upside, she was stylish in dress and demeanor. Her refined manner served to raise the social expectations of the neighborhood. On the downside, Mrs. Robinson was now being seen in public in a condition many felt was under the influence of alcohol or some other drug. The transformation in Mrs. Robinson's behavior was not immediate, but it was swift.

One of the first people Mrs. Robinson approached was a young seamstress named Mary Dillon. What started as a professional relationship between the two women, Mrs. Robinson tried to transform into a friendship. It would not be a pairing of equals.

Mrs. Robinson spoke perfect English and, at the very least, proficient French, while Mary struggled to use the correct verb tense in English. The personal advances of this sophisticated woman were at first welcomed by the seventeen-year-old Mary who found her "manner rather agreeable." To the tales that Mrs. Robinson would spin, Mary was an eager listener. Mary was not sure she believed all of the stories, but the appeal of stories about parties and nobility were compelling to her adolescent fantasies. Their relationship was not long-lived. Eventually Mrs. Robinson's peculiar behavior became too much for the young girl's father. He told Mary to break off the friendship.

It was because of Mary's skill at repairing clothing that Mrs. Robinson first sought her out. In March, Mrs. Robinson went to the Dillon's house on River Street to inquire as to whether Mary could both repair and make alterations to one of her dresses. She wanted the dress lengthened. Once in the Dillon's door, Mrs. Robinson said that she needed the garment at once. Mary begged off, pointing to the piles of mending that lay around the room, saying that she already had too much work. Mary told her potential client that she could not take on anything more, and definitely not a project that needed to be done immediately. After all, shortening clothes is a much simpler process than lengthening them. Mrs. Robinson persisted, saying that she wanted the dress lengthened by letting out the hem in the waist. She also wanted another minor repair done on the dress. Perhaps to pacify her potential customer, Mary examined the garment. With a skilled eye, she looked at the amount of material at the seam at the waist of the dress. Mary turned the dress partially inside out, then pointed out to Mrs. Robinson that there was not enough material left to lengthen the dress, even if she were taking on new projects. Seeing the material for herself, Mrs. Robinson agreed and said that she could live with the dress's length if it were just repaired, referring to the second problem with the dress. Mary looked around the room using her arm as a pointer and said, "I don't know how I can do it right away. I have so much other work."

"I'll pay you any price to have it done.", replied Mrs. Robinson. In one breath she demonstrated that she was not used to waiting or to being denied a request. More importantly, she confirmed that she was used to somehow affording the cost of her needs and wants.

It was in this, the first conversation between the two women, that Mary witnessed Mrs. Robinson's easy aptitude for altering a story, seemingly at will. The uncertainty about Mrs. Robinson's truthfulness was demonstrated on a minor issue with respect to the dress. In explaining the hem in the waist of the dress, at first Mrs. Robinson said that she had cut the dress herself. Later, in the same conversation, she said that the dress had been made by a dressmaker. Mrs. Robinson's trait of relating conflicting information pertaining to a single event was common during the spring of 1853.

Beginning on the day of the request that the dress be sewn, Mrs. Robinson and Mary Dillon were together on several occasions, enjoying prolonged conversations; some of their talks lasted for hours. These encounters were at Mary's house, at Mrs. Robinson's residence, and on walks. There were several pertinent details that came up during these meetings. One topic that was discussed on several different occasions was Mrs. Robinson's background. In one conversation she claimed to be the daughter of an Irish Lord. In that conversation she claimed to have been turned away from her father's castle because she married below her station. When she finished telling the story, Mrs. Robinson began to cry in front of Mary. The tears passed as quickly as they had begun. Mary would later tell how Mrs. Robinson, within minutes of the tears, had "laughed and danced about the floor." As she danced, Mrs. Robinson talked of balls and parties she had attended, as if these events were the source of her merriment. Mrs. Robinson built on the story of her noble birth when, on the next day, she returned to Mary's shop/home with additional clothes that she wanted altered. At this meeting, Mrs. Robinson showed Mary a daguerreotype of a lady with a bouquet of flowers. In looking at the picture, Mary thought it was of a lady about thirty years old. Mrs. Robinson told Mary that the woman was her mother and that the flowers in the picture had been gathered in the garden of the King of France. Mrs. Robinson went on to explain that she had been given the picture by her mother. This was at the same time Mrs. Robinson's own father had turned her away from the family's castle. During this meeting Mrs. Robinson's father switched from being an Irish to a French lord; however, on this same visit Mrs. Robinson said that she was born in Vermont. On yet another occasion Mrs. Robinson told Mary that her mother had died when Mrs. Robinson was a young girl. In this story Mrs. Robinson was turned away from the family home at the request of her stepmother. These changes in facts regarding her background did not put Mary off; instead, she found them intriguing. For a year Mrs. Robinson's background had been the mystery of the neighborhood; why would Mary expect it to be resolved in a few days. Besides, the stories were of a life that Mary had never experienced.

Mrs. Robinson's descriptions of her father were inconsistent. Usually she portrayed him as being very stern and cold. Yet, on at least two occasions, she projected her father as a forgiving person. Once she told Mary that he had sent for her, telling her that he would forgive her for the indiscretions she had committed. In another story, she told Mary that he had sent her $150 to buy a dress to wear when she took Oliver Boutwell to court for slander. There is no evidence that this particular lawsuit ever existed.

The issue surrounding slanderous comments being directed at her became a recurring theme with Mrs. Robinson. Beginning in March, either she became aware that her neighbors were discussing her, or that is when the rumors actually started. In all probability, the neighbors were discussing Mrs. Robinson and her lifestyle from the moment she moved in, but, because of a turn of events, which caused her to come out of the cottage, she suddenly cared about the gossip.

Mrs. Robinson would say many times and to several people that Oliver Boutwell and his family had slandered her name. Since they lived immediately south of Mrs. Robinson, if any one family would know of her behaviors, it would have been the Boutwells. How much the Boutwells discussed her behavior would be pure conjecture; yet to believe that a family, any family, whether it was the Boutwell's or someone else, talked about its neighbors is a reasonable conclusion.

There is another aspect of Mrs. Robinson's background about which she gave Mary two different answers. When she talked of her education, and this was not a topic Mrs. Robinson would broach often, she usually said that she went to "Mrs. Willard's Seminary." This was in fact one of the rumors that ran wild throughout Troy following the double murder. In another conversation, "quite a spell afterwards," the same discussion in which she said that her stepmother wanted her banned from the family estate, Mrs. Robinson spoke of being educated in a nunnery.

When Mary went to Mrs. Robinson's house, the visits lasted for hours. Mary would want to leave, but Mrs. Robinson would not let her go. It was not that she held the young seamstress against her will, but rather that she detained her by persuasion. In an effort to get her young protégé to stay longer, Mrs. Robinson would resort almost to begging. It may have been this compulsive need for companionship that led Mrs. Robinson to expand on her stories.

For two brief weeks, the two women visited daily. During this period, most of the visits took place in Mrs. Robinson's cottage. If Mary would not come to the cottage on her own, Mrs. Robinson would walk to the Dillon's home to get her. The days that the ladies spent together were pleasant, and Mary enjoyed all of the conversations except when Mrs. Robinson began to use profanity. Mrs. Robinson would change her language for no apparent reason. On these occasions, her language was "not the type of ladies."

In addition to Mrs. Robinson's propensity to tell widely divergent stories, she also exhibited some behaviors that Mary found peculiar. One day, in the spring of 1853, Mary and Mrs. Robinson were in the yard watching what was happening on the river. A merchant boat was coming north, up the river. Suddenly, Mrs. Robinson became concerned, saying that the boat would not be able to safely get through the lock because her neighbor, Boutwell, had constructed a dam to divert the water to his mill. When it came out of his sluiceway, the water pushed against the sides of the boats, causing them to be pushed sideways. The lateral movement made it difficult for the boats to enter the lock safely. According to Mary, for some reason, Mrs. Robinson took it upon herself to warn the boat's captain of the impending danger. Mrs. Robinson pulled a revolver from the bodice of her dress and started to climb a slight mound. As she ascended the small hill, gun in hand, she turned to Mary and said, "Wouldn't I make a splendid soldier?" Without ever firing the gun, Mrs. Robinson climbed back down the bank.

Perhaps impressed by her own heroism in pulling the gun, Mrs. Robinson admitted to Mary that she knew how to swim. (Because of issues of modesty and the illnesses associated with water, swimming was not a common skill among women of culture during the Victorian Era.) Mrs. Robinson said that, if she were to swim in the river, she would take along a cork; if she tired, she would put the cork in her mouth and just float and rest for a while.

***

Although all the characters in this play have an air of uniqueness about them, it is Anthony Goodspeed who adds an incredibly masculine imprint. Goodspeed worked as a butcher in the Centre Market in the central part of Troy. It was to this market that Mrs. Robinson had gone on the last day of March. She went to the market in search of game, claiming to be in the mood for wild meat. Goodspeed, who was out of game, made his apologies. He went on to explain that it was the end of the season for game, and it was difficult to come by. Although Mrs. Robinson was only in the store for about fifteen minutes, she asked Goodspeed at least a dozen different times for different types of game. Each time he gave the same answer, that there was none available. As she talked, she walked, seeming to be almost unable to stand in one place.

During the conversation with Goodspeed, Mrs. Robinson said that she had been to the Justice Court to take out a half dozen summons against her neighbors for slandering her name. To Goodspeed, who, from personal experience, would be able to recognize someone under the influence of alcohol, Mrs. Robinson's behaviors were eccentric but not those of someone who was drunk.

There was one final behavior that made her visit stick in Goodspeed's mind. On her way out of the door, Mrs. Robinson remarked that her garter had come undone. She put her boot up on the step, lifted her floor length skirt above her boot and asked Goodspeed to tie her garter for her. In this time, when it was the epitome of bold exposure for or a lady to show a wrist or ankle, to see the entire calf of her leg was flaunting. When Goodspeed finished tying the garter, "round she swirled and off she went."

At about the same time as her visit to the butcher, Mrs. Robinson showed up one night at Mary Dillon's wearing only her nightgown and carrying her pistol. Mrs. Robinson told Mary that a group of ruffians were outside her home, threatening her and trying to force her from the neighborhood. Mrs. Robinson told Mary that she was so frightened that she had to run from her house in the night clothes. Mary was able to calm down Mrs. Robinson. Mary loaned Mrs. Robinson one of her everyday broadcloth dresses to wear home, but Mary refused to walk to the police station with her.

It was after this incident that Mr. Dillon, Mary's father, told his daughter that she could not visit with Mrs. Robinson any more. The factors that caused this gun and night clothes incident requires additional explanation.

In March it was not just with Mary that Mrs. Robinson began to open up. In either the last week in March or the first week in April, the Lanagans decided to have a dance at their store. There were two purposes for hosting a dance. First and foremost, a dance would provide an opportunity for a little revelry among the neighbors. Second, the Lanagans could use the extra cash that could be raised by charging an admission. These dances were referred to as 'kitchen dances' and were commonly held among the labor class. The kitchen dance was the counterpart to the barn dance held in the rural countryside. For those who attended these dances, they were a venue where people could mix. Even then, the idea that a romance could potentially develop was a sign of spring.

Having operated the store for six months, Mrs. Lanagan knew everyone who attended the dance, except one young man named David Smith. Smith boarded in a house south of the store on River Street. He probably came to the dance either as an associate of one of the Lanagans' friends, or, less likely, he had come on his own, seeking companionship.

Mrs. Robinson came by the store while the dance was going on, ostensibly to buy some supplies. Hearing the noise and watching the gaiety, Mrs. Robinson decided to remain and to socialize with her neighbors, something she would not have done prior to March. David Smith came over to Mrs. Robinson and struck up a conversation. He did so either on the basis of physical attraction or on the basis of the community's understanding of her background. During the Victorian Era, women who had shared their affection without the benefit of marriage did not necessarily make suitable wives, but they were popular company among the rowdy young men of most towns. In the spirit of the evening, or because he was in to the spirits, David asked Mrs. Robinson to dance. She refused his offer. David did not take rejections lightly and proceeded to call Mrs. Robinson names. Mrs. Robinson reached into the bodice of her dress and pulled out a revolver. She pointed the hand gun at Smith and ordered him to cease his comments or, as she put it, she would, "Blow his brains out!"

At this point Timothy Lanagan interceded, saying he would have "no such noise." In an effort to quell the situation, Mrs. Lanagan joined her husband in telling Mrs. Robinson that she needed to leave and in offering to accompany her home. As Mrs. Robinson reluctantly walked home, she told Mrs. Lanagan that she felt molested by Smith. Mrs. Lanagan told her, "If you keep to your own place, no one will molest you." It was after dark and the portly Mrs. Lanagan walked the shapely Mrs. Robinson all the way to the door of her residence.

When Anna Lanagan returned to the dance, she believed that the incident was over. A little later that evening, Mrs. Robinson returned to the store, but she only came as far as the door. She asked of the person who came to the door to have David Smith come outside. Smith left the dance, and no one saw either of them again that evening.

It was either the next morning, or the morning after, that the first disagreement between Mrs. Robinson and the Lanagans took place. Mrs. Robinson went to the store early in the morning. Mrs. Lanagan was working in the store alone, since her husband was still asleep. Mrs. Robinson immediately became abusive, saying that Anna Lanagan was a "mean" person who allowed "rowdies" into her house. Demonstrating how personally she took these events, Mrs. Robinson implied that these rowdies were there expressly to insult her.

In what on the surface would be considered one of those threats made in anger, Mrs. Robinson went on to say that she, "would have them (the Lanagans) turned out of their place.", and that she had the power and would use it to see that they "did not have a license to sell." Coercion of this type, made in anger, was fairly common then as it is now. The difference is that, in Mrs. Robinson's case, she may have had the connections to follow through on such a threat. With the rumors that were afoot about her and her powerful connections, the Lanagans would have known that she could possibly become a dangerous adversary. They would have feared her power far more than the loss of her trade.

Mrs. Lanagan would later tell the story as though she were the relentless mediator, saying that she had responded, "I want no trouble with you.", adding, "just go home."

Hearing the commotion, Timothy Lanagan arose and went into the store. He was less tolerant than his wife. He said to Mrs. Robinson, "I will have not such noise.", adding that she had to leave the store.

Mrs. Robinson refused to leave. In angered tones, she asked why he would want to turn away such a good customer. She had been in the practice of visiting the store daily since she began personally trading at the Lanagan's, but, if he did not back off, she would shop in another store.

Her threat did not scare Timothy Lanagan, and he indicated to her that, if those were his two options, he did want her "custom", but instead he wanted her to leave. Mrs. Robinson refused to depart and told Lanagan, "If you want me out, you will have to call a constable."

Again Mrs. Lanagan would claim to have interceded to bring peace to the situation. She said that she sent her husband back into the residence of the building while she talked to Mrs. Robinson alone. Eventually, cooler heads prevailed, and Mrs. Robinson left. Mrs. Robinson made good on her threat and did not trade at the Lanagans' for about three weeks after this fight.

It was at about the same time as the incident at the dance that Mrs. Robinson showed up at Mary Dillon's dressed only in her night clothes and carrying a pistol. It is very probable that the events happened in one night. The evening would have begun with Mrs. Robinson going uninvited to the dance, followed by her tempting Smith to go outside for a confrontation. It is quite probable that a group of men who had been at the dance went to her home after the dance in an effort to intimidate Mrs. Robinson into moving. She then left her home, running to the Dillon's in her night clothes. The sequence of events concluded with the disagreement with the Lanagans.

Within a few days of May 10, Mrs. Robinson made a fateful visit to the drugstore operated by William Ostrom, on the corner of Federal and River Street in center Troy. This was several blocks south of where Mrs. Robinson lived. She frequented the store often during the month of May, 1853, perhaps to keep an eye out for her lover (this possibility will be examined later). Her objective this day was to purchase arsenic. Mrs. Robinson told Ostrom that she needed the poison because of an infestation of rats attracted to her neighborhood by Boutwell's Mill. Ostrom was aware of the problem and sold her two ounces of arsenic. Ostrom divided the arsenic into two piles, which he wrapped in separate white paper packages. Each paper package of arsenic was clearly marked "poison". She paid for the arsenic in cash; if she had put it on credit, Ostrom would have recorded the sale in his day book, and he would then have given the exact day of the sale. She purchased the poison a full two weeks before the double murder.

Mrs. Robinson was in the drug store again on the Saturday evening prior to the poisoning. While she was there, Ostrom could not help noticing her demeanor. Her skin was flushed, and she used language which was much bolder than he was used to hearing from her. Although he assumed she was under the influence of alcohol, he thought the symptoms she exhibited might be from extreme anxiety. Ostrom noticed what appeared to be the barrel of a handgun protruding from the bodice of her dress. He inquired about what he saw, and Mrs. Robinson took the revolver from her dress and handed it to Ostrom. She told Ostrom that she carried the weapon because of concern for her safety. She felt that a group of young men in her neighborhood meant to do her harm. Ostrom poked down one of the barrels with a pen, assuring himself that the gun was loaded. He looked at the hammer and noticed that three or four percussion caps had been stacked on top of each other instead of the one that was required. Ostrom was able to see extensive rust around the metal hammer and believed that there was no way the gun could actually be used. He gave the gun back to Mrs. Robinson, sure that it could do no harm.

Ostrom told Mrs. Robinson that the police were responsible

for maintaining the peace and that if, in fact, she was concerned about her safety, she should have them patrol more frequently. Ostrom went so far as to say that the chief might even send a posse of officers to protect her.

***

Mrs. Robinson's impression that she was being threatened by rowdies from her neighborhood was a very real possibility. It was not uncommon at this time, when people were actually out of their homes and more visible to their neighbors, for neighbor to turn against neighbor. If someone in a neighborhood was considered to be "undesirable", the other residents would gather together in an effort to push the person out. When one of these expulsions was under way, screaming, name-calling, knocking on windows, and other threatening behavior was very much the norm. Women and older people would shun the "outcast", making him avoid coming out in public. Parents would rarely discipline their sons for obnoxiously rowdy behavior directed against an "undesirable". Young women would cross the street or turn away, making the person feel transparent. Young men would gather near the person's home making threatening gestures and comments, often under the cover of darkness. A woman with a reputation similar to Mrs. Robinson could easily expect that the neighbors would not want her to remain. The complaint that Mrs. Robinson related to Ostrom was, in all probability, true. As will become evident, the event in March that triggered Mrs. Robinson's transition to an active member of the community also removed her protection from her neighbors.

***

Edwin Brownell, Overseer of the Poor, worked in an office in the basement of the courthouse. For some unexplained reason, in May of 1853, he decided that he had to work late one Sunday evening (the date was probably May 10). By 7:30, it was dark, yet Brownell was still at work in his office. Unannounced, two men he had never seen before came into his office and announced that a lady was there to see him. A gracious civil servant, Brownell asked that they leave the door open and tell the lady to come in. He waited, and no one entered. Hearing sounds in the hallway, he walked to his door. The hallway was so dark that Brownell needed to light a gas lamp to see anything. As the flame grew in brightness, he noticed a woman standing in the shadows. He extended his arm in a gesture indicating direction and asked her to come into his office and to take a seat. The woman staggered a little bit on her way down the hall to the office. Brownell was not sure if her lack of coordination was the result of drinking or of the darkness. He assumed it was from alcohol. He was not sure of the woman's identity, but he had seen her on the streets of Troy. He also believed that he recognized her from five or six years earlier when she had lived in Troy. The woman did possess a sort of presence that would make her stick in a person's mind.

It was a mistake that the woman was in his office. The lady, who did not identify herself, asked Brownell if he was the Chief of Police. Brownell said he was not, adding that the man she wanted was Mr. Coop, whose office was near the jail. Brownell assured her that, if she went to the Chief's office, she would probably find him. The woman replied that it would be difficult for her to find the office in the dark, implying that he should accompany her. Brownell begged off, saying that he had work to do before he could leave. She told him that she wanted the Chief because she was having trouble with some of her neighbors. After telling Brownell exactly where she lived, she told him that she wanted the Chief to send an officer to protect her house.

Realizing that this woman was not going to leave his office until the matter was resolved, Brownell walked to the Chief's office. Not finding him there, he went to the Chief's residence, which was nearby. He told the Chief about his uninvited guest, telling the Chief her name and her problem. The chief seemed to recognize the name and told Brownell to walk her home, promising to send an officer to protect her home.

When Brownell returned to his office, the woman was still sitting in the same chair. He offered to walk her home, but she remained seated and proceeded to tell him about the problems that she was experiencing. The problems seemed to focus on two men, David Smith, and a man named Gillespie. She explained how they had broken into her home. To Brownell, the woman seemed to be very genuine in her fears.

It was during the second part of the conversation that the

true source of her fear and the depth of her influence emerged. She asked Brownell if he was acquainted with Canal Commissioner John C. Mather, who lived in Troy. Brownell was proud to acknowledge that he knew Mather. To live in Troy and to have any political aspirations meant that you had to know Mather; after all, his name had been seriously considered for nomination to be a candidate for Governor the previous October. Much more will be said about Mather later.

The woman asked whether Brownell knew Mather's whereabouts. She was concerned that Mather had not been paying attention to her of late. Brownell said he was sure that Mather, who was the Canal Commissioner, was attending to Canal business. He was sure that Mather was either checking on the breaks that happened every winter, or, perhaps, was in Washington.

As the conversation changed direction, the woman's emotional level increased. She asked Brownell if he had heard the rumor that Mather was now engaged to Judge Geer's daughter. Brownell told her that he had not heard that rumor. The woman then told Brownell that Mather could not marry Miss Geer, because she was already Mather's legal wife. The lady told Brownell that she and Mather had been married in his father's house the previous year. In a cool calculated voice, the woman said that when Mather returned, she would make him avow to the marriage, or she would take his life.

The lady sat in Brownell's office for over an hour. During that time, there was a heavy rain outside. Eventually, Brownell was able to talk the lady into letting him walk her home. Brownell remembered that she lived in a small cottage near the river, adjacent to Boutwell's large home. When he got to the house, the woman showed him two handguns. He examined them carefully. He loaded two barrels of one so that the lady would feel secure. Then he left her house, reassuring her that an officer would be nearby.

Brownell's interest was peaked. The next day he made inquiries regarding Mather's whereabouts. Brownell learned, through credible sources, that Mather was in Washington.

On the following Saturday night (May 16), Brownell was walking on the streets of Central Troy at about 9:00 in the evening. He noticed a woman across the street on the arm of a much older man. If she had not visited his office the week before, Brownell probably would not have recognized or even noticed the woman. He could not help noticing what he thought was a disguise. She had on a full bonnet, which covered the sides of her face, and clothes that seemed too big for her. The location where Brownell sighted her was significant; she was within a few buildings of Mather's boarding house.

Although she never introduced herself, Brownell was sure that the woman who came to his office and the woman he saw on the street was known by the name of Mrs. Robinson.

There are families to be born into, and there are names and legacies to be avoided. Unfortunately, people do not have any choice and end up where chance puts them. In the Victorian era, there were not many families in Troy with a better history than the Knickerbackers. John Knickerbacker was from a fine old Dutch family that by 1850 could trace its roots in the Hudson Valley back 200 years. A single man, Knickerbacker lived in Mrs. Brewster's boarding house at 102 Second Street; this was the same address as John C. Mather.

On the evening of May 23, (a week after the sighting by Brownell) between 10 and 11 p.m., John Knickerbacker was walking down Congress Street. He could not help noticing a droll-looking woman walking on the arm of a very old man. Her light spirit amused Knickerbacker. As they reached the corner of Second Street, the woman asked Knickerbacker if he knew the location of Mrs. Brewster's boarding house. While they were in the glow of a gas light, he pointed out the boarding house. He was impressed by how excited she appeared to be. Like Ostrom, who had seen her earlier in the evening, Knickerbacker did not think she had been drinking any form of intoxicants. Knickerbacker followed the lady and old man down the street in the direction of Ferry Street. In an effort to observe the unusual couple, he turned down the side street just a little but kept himself in a position to see Mrs. Brewster's door. The couple stood in front of the boarding house for a few seconds, then the old man went up and rang the bell. When no one answered, he returned to the woman, who had waited on the sidewalk. To Knickerbacker, they seemed to talk, then she went up and rang the bell. Again no one came to the door, so the couple left, turning back in the direction of Knickerbacker.

The woman and old man turned around, walking from the direction in which they had come. They turned a second time and came up the side street where Knickerbacker had taken up reconnoitering. Given the options of walking away or directly toward the couple, Knickerbacker decided it would be wise to just walk forward, and started in the direction of his boarding house. As the woman was passing, she drew a pistol from the bodice of her dress and pointed it in the direction of Knickerbacker. She said in a clear voice, "You see I am prepared not to be followed."

The woman turned out to be Mrs. Robinson. This occurred on the day Mather returned to the city from Washington.

That Fateful Day

It is important to examine the movements of Mrs. Robinson on May 25, 1853. The reader needs to keep in mind that the following account is based on the statement from Catherine Lubbee, comments made by Timothy Lanagan to the doctors who treated him, but primarily on statements made by Mrs. Lanagan, the only witness who survived.

On that fateful day, Mrs. Robinson went to Lanagan's store on five different occasions. Although the neighborhood store was a place to meet and to congregate, five visits in one day would have to be considered to be out of the norm. Her first trip was at six in the morning when she crossed the street to purchase a quart of strong beer and some crackers, which gives some indication of how she had spent the previous evening. At the time of this visit, Timothy Lanagan had not arisen yet, but Mrs. Lanagan had opened the store. Anna sold Mrs. Robinson the two items that she requested, recording the sale in the accounts register. With artificial light at such a premium, people managed their lives around daylight. Six in the morning may sound early today, but would have been a common time for a grocery in 1853.

Approximately two hours later, Mrs. Robinson sent her gardener, Old-Man-Haley, to the store to borrow two dollars. Mrs. Robinson, like many of her neighbors, was in the practice of borrowing cash from the Lanagans. The amount borrowed was always added to her account. More importantly, she was in the habit of repaying the loans promptly. On this occasion, Mrs. Lanagan asked Old-Man-Haley about the purpose of the loan. The elderly man responded that he was not sure why Mrs. Robinson needed the two dollars, since she had everything she needed in the house. When Old-Man-Haley did not return in a timely fashion, Mrs. Robinson went to the store to inquire about the delay.

"What has kept you so long?", demanded Mrs. Robinson of Haley.

Before he could answer, Mrs. Lanagan responded, "I kept him." She went on to explain, "I have no money in the house, and I was wondering if I should send for some cash."

Mrs. Robinson inquired, "Are you so scarce of cash?"

"Yes.", was Mrs. Lanagan's retort.

Perhaps suspecting an untruth, Mrs. Robinson countered, "If you have no money, tomorrow I will lend you $100." These words would be interpreted very differently if one imagines that they were said sarcastically or, instead, if they were said with sincerity. There is no interpretation given, but, based on her recent dealings with some others in the neighborhood, sarcasm is a distinct possibility. In any event, Mrs. Robinson left with Old-Man-Haley but without the money.

Later, Mrs. Lanagan would admit that she was lying at the time, and that she did in fact have the two dollars in the house. For some unexplained reason, on this occasion she chose not to lend cash to Mrs. Robinson.

Mrs. Robinson's third visit to the Lanagan's was at about eleven that morning. When she came in this time, she said that she was in great trouble. "I just received a telegram and Mr. Robinson has been hurt on the cars!" The term "on the cars" refers to the railroad.

A man, Welch, was in the store at the time. He tried to relieve some of the anxiety or add levity by saying, "My wife is in the west and I would not fret until I saw her.", an obvious reference to a feeling that he feared his wife's presence more than her injury.

Timothy Lanagan was downtown on an errand at the time of the eleven o'clock visit. A portion of his trip included a visit to Morrison & Lord's, a grocery and butcher's shop. While in

Lanagans' store, Mrs. Robinson could hear commotion from the back room of the store/house, and, without being invited, she went into the kitchen to see what was happening. There were several men in the back room apparently playing cards. When Mrs. Robinson went in the kitchen, the men's voices grew louder in that way that was common when a group of men felt that their space had been invaded by an uninvited woman. After a few minutes, Mrs. Robinson left the men to their conversation, returning to the store. Within a few more minutes, Mrs. Robinson returned to the back room. This time the noise was too much for her host. Mrs. Lanagan went into the room and told Mrs. Robinson that, "You need to go home." She looked over her shoulder as she hustled Mrs. Robinson from the room, adding, "It is no place for you to be among such a lot of men." In the language of the day, the word "lot" did not necessarily mean quantity, but could also refer to a negative value. "Such at lot of men" in this context probably meant that they had the tendency to become rowdy and troublesome.

It was a little after one in the afternoon when Mrs. Robinson entered the Lanagans' store for the fourth time. When she came into the store, no one was in the front room. This neighborhood being as informal as it was, Mrs. Robinson walked through the store and entered the back room. There she found Mr. and Mrs. Lanagan and Catherine Lubbee finishing their lunch. Seeing that they were finishing, she politely asked a rhetorical question, "Are you at dinner?"

"Yes", was the answer provided by Mrs. Lanagan.

Mrs. Robinson looked at the table and noticed that there was an egg and a potato that had not been eaten. She asked, "Whose egg is that?"

"It's yours if you want it.", responded Mr. Lanagan, as he rose from his seat, preparing to return to his duties in the store.

Mrs. Robinson took the warm seat Lanagan had vacated and took the hard boiled egg up in her hand. As Mrs. Robinson started to eat the egg, Mrs. Lanagan rose, went to the stove, and took a potato out of the pot. She peeled the potato for Mrs. Robinson, then returned to her seat at the table. The three women talked in quiet tones as Mrs. Robinson finished her simple lunch. While Mrs. Robinson was eating her eggs and potato, Mrs. Lanagan thought she saw a small piece of white paper in her hand.

When the meal was over, Mrs. Robinson appeared to want

to make restitution; she offered, "You ladies must have a glass of beer on my account."

"I don't want any.", responded Mrs. Lanagan, going on to say, "I'm tired of beer." There would later be a debate as to whether Mrs. Lanagan was willing to accept the purchase of a brandy in replacement for the beer. There was a parallel story in which Mrs. Lanagan had taken a glass of brandy in lieu of the beer.

Catherine's response to the offer was, "I don't much like beer."

In an effort to make the beer more palatable, Mrs. Robinson requested of Mrs. Lanagan, "Have you any sugar in the house?"

"Yes", but you don't want any; you just got nine pounds last week." responded Mrs. Lanagan, misunderstanding Mrs. Robinson's intent.

Mrs. Robinson smiled as she continued, "I don't want it to take home." There was a tone in her voice as if to say that Mrs. Lanagan was being silly. "I want to put it in the beer to make it good." Without standardized brewing requirements, beer of this period could, and often did, have a bitter quality.

Finally grasping the intent for the sugar, Mrs. Lanagan took a saucer and went into the store. She returned minutes later with a saucer covered with white sugar. Mrs. Lanagan then returned to the store and pulled a quart measure of beer from the tap. Mrs. Lanagan must have meant to take one glass, or she was expecting Catherine to drink a lot of a substance that she did not like. When Mrs. Lanagan returned to the back room, she saw Mrs. Robinson pacing the floor with the saucer of sugar in her hand. Mrs. Lanagan poured the beer into two tumblers. The beer did not fill the tumblers, so Mrs. Robinson said, "I will have these two glasses full." Mrs. Lanagan returned to the store and pulled enough beer to fill the tumblers. When Mrs. Lanagan returned to the back room, she witnessed Mrs. Robinson pouring the sugar into the beer. Mrs. Lanagan then poured enough beer from the second measure to fill the tumblers.

As Mrs. Lanagan sat down at the table, there were two glasses of beer. One was in front of Mrs. Lanagan, and the other in front of Catherine. Mrs. Lanagan noticed a white powder on the top of her beer. Thinking it was dust from the sugar, she took a spoon to scoop it off. Mrs. Robinson took the spoon out of Mrs. Lanagan's hand, saying, "Don't you do so, that is the best of it." (The existence of the powder on the top of the beer was discussed earlier in this book.)

There would later be a question as to whether Mrs. Robinson had any beer herself. There would have been some left from the second measure. There was one report, and only one, that Mrs. Robinson claimed that she did drink some and that, like Lanagan and Lubbee, it made her sick. Mrs. Lanagan neither denied that Mrs. Robinson had some nor confirmed it, saying that she did not know what became of the remaining beer.

According to Mrs. Lanagan, before she could actually taste the beer, her husband called to her from inside the store. She got up and went through the doorway to see what he wanted. Lanagan told his wife that he wanted to go downtown on some errands, and that he wanted her to handle the store while he was gone. As Mrs. Lanagan went to the front of the store, Lanagan went into the back room and picked up his wife's beer. A few minutes later, Mrs. Robinson left the store without any further conversation with Mrs. Lanagan.

Mr. Lanagan came out from the back room and entered some sales into his account book before leaving to go downtown. While he was busy recording in his book, Catherine came to the door and asked, "How do you feel?"

"Not very comfortable," was his response. This exchange was after the two had finished their beer and after Mrs. Robinson had left the building.

The fifth visit by Mrs. Robinson was at approximately three o'clock. This visit occurred at the time Lanagan returned from downtown and was reported in the opening of this book.

Troy Female Seminary

Jail

David Wilson

In the 1850's there lived an author in the Capital District who had published two historical biographies about regional characters. The author, David Wilson, was a politician, lawyer and the editor/publisher of a newspaper in Whitehall. In 1855, Wilson released a third book entitled *Henrietta Robinson*. According to Wilson's preface, he was convinced to write his account by "several eminent legal gentlemen." The "gentlemen's" interests were in having a record of what they thought was a clear rendering "of the law as laid down by the judge." He was referring to the charge to the jury, made by Judge Ira Harris in the trial of Mrs. Robinson. As it turned out, Wilson's narrative would play into the political plans of at least one of the principal characters in the trial. While completing his research and writing the book, Wilson became consumed by the same two aspects of this case that the community at large desired to know. He spent most of his efforts trying to determine the identity of Mrs. Robinson and to ascertain her sanity.

Wilson was not selected at random to tell this story. In 1853, he had two books released. Wilson helped Solomon Northup write his book, *12 Years a Slave*. Northup, an African-American, was born a freeman and lived most of his life in the area of Glens Falls, New York. While in his 30's, Northup was enticed into going into Washington, DC, where he was drugged and sold into slavery. The first person who purchased Northup was a slave trader who moved him south to be sold a second time. Ultimately, he was sold to an owner in Louisiana where he spent twelve years working on a plantation. When Wilson started to write Mrs. Robinson's story, he was still basking in the sales of Northup's story, which would ultimately sell 30,000 copies. It is worthy of note that Northup's account is considered to be one of the most accurate portrayals of life as a slave in America. Northup's story came out at nearly the same time as *Uncle Tom's Cabin* by Harriett Beacher Stowe. Like Stowe's book, Northup's account contributed greatly to the sentiments of the north against slavery. In the same year as the Northup book, Wilson released an account of the life of Jane McCrea, a martyr in the Revolutionary War.

In very many ways, Wilson's version of Henrietta

Robinson's, saga is essential to our ability to understand the story today. Wilson had several advantages as an author of this tale; Wilson wrote the story of Mrs. Robinson's while it was still unfolding. The book was published just after the story was thought to have concluded. (As will be shown later, the story probably did not end when Wilson thought.) As a contemporary of those who were involved in the story, Wilson was able to interview some of those who knew Mrs. Robinson. Probably because of the political power of those who induced him to record the story, he was able to question people who were not even called as witnesses. One of the most important interviews conducted by Wilson was that of Mrs. Robinson's lover, or his emissary. Equally fascinating is Wilson's admission in his preface that he was actually able to meet Mrs. Robinson in person on at least one occasion. Through his sources, Wilson was able to report information that cannot be corroborated by other documents such as the records of the trial or the accounts in the newspapers. Wilson, of course suffered two key disadvantages over a reporter today. Writing his book as a current event deprived him of perspectives that can only be gained by space and time. Additionally, he was unable to write about the extremely interesting follow-up to the story.

Although it lacks the perspective of the political and social issues, Wilson's version should still be considered valuable and reasonable from a factual standpoint. The accuracy of Wilson's books on Jane McCrea and Northup show that he was consumed by insuring that the facts in his accounts were correct. The book about Northup was researched in the 1970's by a group of professors from Louisiana State University. These professors were able to use other sources such as newspaper accounts and court records to demonstrate that the Northup account was incredibly accurate. It is within this context that Wilson's record of Henrietta Robinson needs to be considered.

Wilson fell short in the political aspects of the incident. As a fellow politician who worked with the people in his book, he was careful to protect their identities. One of the best examples of Wilson's care is evident in the numerous instances in which he drew a line instead of placing an actual name of a cohort or politically-connected individual. At other times he would give only hints to an identity, such as that of a man who was once famous on the national scene but who had since fallen from grace (Van Buren). Using newspaper accounts, the identities can usually be determined, but when his book was published, it would have been difficult for someone who was not from this area to obtain copies of the old newspapers.

The origin of the problem with Wilson's account lies in the very nature of his becoming involved in the case; he was drawn in because there were those who wanted to convey a political message. Some of Wilson's facts cannot be corroborated because they were not brought out in the trial or in newspaper accounts. The fact that he learned of a story or fact that neither the newspapers nor the trial covered implies that someone wanted that incident revealed. These personal sources of Wilson placed a weight on his perceptions and, inevitably, biased his version. This does not mean that his facts are incorrect, only that their interpretation is inevitably weighted. Since the facts are important, wherever Wilson is the only source, it is noted in the text.

***

If the story of Mrs. Robinson is to be truly understood, it must be viewed at many levels. Because of the time period and the reason Wilson gave for his narrative, only some of the many facets were covered in his work. There are the obvious three stories of the tragic murders, the related search for the identity of Mrs. Robinson, and the question of her sanity, which Wilson covered. There are three other facets not covered by Wilson. They are the political level, social level, and the ultimate outcomes of the individuals involved in the case.

Because he was living within the values of the time, Wilson missed the deeper story relating to the social structure. Although this story is about Troy, in many ways this city was a reflection of cities in the northeast, if not in America as a whole. In the Robinson story, the lives of recent immigrants, who are existing in an environment in which six people lived in one room, are being controlled by men who lived in mansions and who proudly traced their roots to the first boats to New England. Virtually all of the members of both legal teams were able to trace their roots to soldiers, usually officers, in the American Revolution. In their own way, these men were America's nobility.

For reasons that will be explained later in detail, it would have been politically imprudent for Wilson to explore the political ramifications of this trial. Many of the men in this trial were members of a vast political machine. This machine was so powerful and vengeful that to expose its weak underside would have been political suicide for Wilson. It may also have meant that Wilson's book would probably never have been published.

The final facet that Wilson could not have covered was the ultimate impact of Mrs. Robinson on the lives of those involved. In fairness, it would have been impossible for Wilson to have guessed the course that this boat of destiny was to follow.

During the trial, three sides of the complex web of the political infrastructure of New York were on the line. Those involved in the trial represented all segments of this political dilemma. These political issues were playing heavily on the minds of the men involved in the events of this story. More importantly, those involved represented each political aspect the defense, prosecution, and judge were selected exactly along political party lines. The United States and New York State were going through a redefinition of the political parties. The Whigs were on their way out. The Republican Party was in development. The national Democratic Party was deeply split over how to handle the issue of the expansion of slavery into the territories.

In this one story we have:

- Judge Harris, a future U.S. senator (who becomes the close personal friend of a president)
- Attorney Beach, the college classmate of the governor, Seymour (the same man would later defend numerous politicians on charges of fraud)
- Mather, the first public servant impeached in New York (he was not convicted)
- Attorney Hogeboom, a man who was, at the time of the trial, contesting his failure to be elected a supreme court judge, (an independent inquiry found that the election was probably stolen from him)
- Beach, Townsend, Pierson, and Hogeboom, four former

district attorneys (they represented both political parties)
- Mather, one of the most powerful commissioners in the state (the canals had made New York the Empire State)
- Several congressmen
- Numerous Assemblymen and State Senators
- Jennyss, the police magistrate for Troy
- Townsend, a man who would serve for many years on the Board of Regents

Probably the best example of this overlapping of political roles was the author himself. While David Wilson was writing the book he was an Assemblyman. He knew intimately each of the men involved in this trial. Young enough to still want a political career and beholding to the very men who would become involved in this story, Wilson could not have been truly objective. Wilson was rewarded for his loyalty; he went on to be the Clerk for the Assembly.

It is the intent of this narrative to relate the multiple layers of this tale in a meaningful way while avoiding the traps confronted by Wilson.

Who Was Mrs. Robinson
Part I

Two stories about Henrietta Robinson that predate May 25, 1853, appear in David Wilson's book. Near the beginning of the book, without citing his sources or naming her family, Wilson relates Mrs. Robinson's background and her family life until the time she moved back to the Capital District in about 1850. In the two stories, he gives details in a florid language expected in the Victorian Era but frowned upon today. Near the end of the book, he provides the name of Mrs. Robinson's family. The following is a summary of the first of these stories.

The woman known in Troy as Mrs. Robinson was born in the city of Quebec, Canada, in 1827. She would have been 26 at the time of the double poisoning. She was born to wealth and social grace. Her father had amassed a fortune in the lumber industry and was the patriarch of one of the most successful families in the

Canadian Province. Until she was sixteen, she lived in her father's mansion, which graced the shores of the Saint Lawrence River. In a time when families were measured by their propriety, her wealthy family moved in "the most refined circles of society." In the morally upright Victorian Era, her family was respected for its integrity and were proud always to have maintained an "honorable name." She was born into a family that already had the status that ambitious and entrepreneurial Americans sought.

Until she was sixteen, the woman known as Mrs. Robinson was educated in her father's home. Financially able to hire tutors, her father had provided years of education in his home for all five of his daughters. In 1843, she and one of her younger sisters were sent to the female Seminary at Troy (Emma Willard). She attended the Seminary for two years, applying herself in the visual arts and music. She also studied French and, by the time she graduated, was considered to be fluent in the language (Quebec was a bilingual province even then, and she probably had a passing skill at the language when she arrived at Troy). Her behavior at the academy was excellent, as indicated by the fact that she never "incurred any disapprobation."

In addition to her outstanding financial birthright, she was also had been blessed with physical attractiveness. She was of medium height, with coal black hair, dark blue eyes, and an unusual degree of natural beauty. In fact, some of the men of Troy who knew her when she was sixteen years old, described her as having "a complexion fairer than art can imitate, and teeth whiter than the snows of her native north." (an example of Wilson's style) She stood erect, with a carriage enhanced by the same sense of pride that had pushed her to be outstanding in her academic studies. With her father's wealth came a wardrobe that was both stylish and made of the best materials. She was the type of woman who, by her very presence, was assured that she was noticed wherever she went.

Like many of those blessed with an above-average charisma, and who are forced to exhibit a bright and generous side, there harbored below the surface a dark side waiting to emerge. In the case of the woman known as Henrietta Robinson, these indulgences had two facets – justice and anger. She had a sense of justice that showed itself most often when she rejected expectations placed upon her that she felt were unfair. Even worse, as a girl she showed evidence of her wild side and was known for "the most frightful and fiery passions." So famous were her fits of anger that it was described in whispers as "excitable in the extreme."

By the time of the trial, when people discussed Henrietta, there were questions raised about her moral sense going all the way back to when she was an adolescent in Troy. That would be easy to understand; after all, this is the story of a woman accused of a double murder who had been the mistress of a famous man. To question her morality was a natural human tendency. The story of Mrs. Robinson was the type that families recited over and over to their daughters to keep them from wanting to go to the evil cities.

There are two stories dating from her days at the seminary that Wilson thought were examples of her propensity toward insanity. In one, she commissioned the making of an oversized doll. When the doll was done, she sat it in a chair in her room. She sent out invitations to her classmates inviting them to a party at which she introduced the doll with "great ceremony and formality." Although this may have been an early example of her mental state, there is every possibility that this action was just a prank or a rebellion against the strict social code that was part of the expectations of the Seminary at that time.

In the second incident, Mrs. Robinson and a group of fellow students went to a pond to go swimming. She supposedly went in too deep and had to be rescued. In the 1840's, the clothes that women wore when they went swimming were heavy and would have pulled down even a good swimmer. Wilson states that, when he talked to her in jail, she told him that she wished the water had been allowed to take her life, rather than to have found herself in the predicament she now faced. While this may be another example of mental illness, it is doubtful that many women in jail, awaiting trial for murder, did not think that an earlier death might not have been preferable.

While attending the seminary, there were many socials at which she met several young men. There was, however, one man from Troy who totally caught her fancy. Like her, he was intelligent, educated, and congenial with a promising future. Unlike her, he was of a middle class family. Her parents had aspirations for her marriage into a more refined family. Discovering that their daughter was emotionally involved with a commoner, the family brought her back to Quebec, hoping that separation would break the emotional attraction that had been created. At the beginning of her stay in Quebec, the two young lovers secretly wrote to each other. Eventually her parents were proven right, and time and distance ended the contacts.

Stationed in Canada at the time of her return was a young man who was a member of the British Cavalry Guard. This man's background matched her parents' desires; after all, "he had wealth" and "aristocratic connections". If not for the young man in Troy, his reputation as a sportsman and rider, combined with refined manner and reasonable looks, might have proven sufficient for even this rebellious daughter. Instead, when he proposed, she confessed her love for another. She went on to tell him how their union would fail. Despite her claims of love for another, she was pressured by her family to accept his proposal. On December 16, 1846, the two married. Wilson's description of the young woman's perception of her marriage ceremony was flowery in the extreme; he said that she saw the service as offering "herself as a reckless and haughty sacrifice on the alter of world pride." If Mrs. Robinson did use language such as this during his interview, then the Seminary could be proud of their language program.

The honeymoon was a trip to the young officer's family home in England. Since it was winter, the couple traveled first to Montreal then south to New York City, where they boarded a ship for Liverpool. It was in Montreal that her new husband first experienced her fiery side. Angry and frustrated, she dressed in men's clothes and walked through the streets, stopping frequently in bars, where she drank more than she should. She spent the entire evening raving at her husband.

When they reached England, they went immediately to his family home in London. To her surprise, this home was larger than her father's grand estate in Canada. For three years the couple lived a resentful and unhappy life. To those they entertained, the relationship appeared normal; however, those able to see through the bitter couple's mask could see the effect that the stress was having on both of them. In an effort to pacify her notorious temper, her husband took her on an excursion to the tranquility of the Scottish Highlands. When that did not rectify the situation, he took her to the excitement of Paris, where he hoped the social life would placate her. Still not satisfied, the two went to Italy and the south of France. During their travels, her feelings for her husband went from apathy to loathing.

During the same three years they were together in Europe, she bore her husband two children. Per the social custom of the day, these children would have been raised in most part by a governess.

By 1849 she had made up her mind that the living arrangements had deteriorated from unpleasant to intolerable. Knowing she could no longer maintain a gracious face to society, plans were made that fall to travel back to her family in Canada. There is a question as to whether her husband knew of her desire to leave or whether the entire excursion was surreptitious. In any event, the dejected wife, accompanied on her voyage by her French maid, Helen Reynaud, left Manchester, England, bound for New York City. There is reason to believe that her husband did not know of her plans, as she would later tell Wilson that she stayed close to her cabin "suspecting there were spies on the vessel." There is equal reason to believe that the woman stayed close to the cabin because she admitted that both she and the maid were seasick for virtually the entire passage.

When she arrived in New York City, the lady and her maid stayed in the stylish Irving House. It took the woman and her maid a couple of days to recuperate from their shipboard illness before they felt that they could continue their trip north to her family's home in Quebec.

When they were well enough, the two women booked passage on a Hudson River steamer. The first leg of the trip ended in Troy, where the woman walked the familiar streets that had played such an important part of the two happy years she had spent as a student at the Seminary. She was back in a place of warm memories. She found herself feeling the early surges of peace and tranquility that she had missed during her marriage. She had aged and matured, allowing her to visit her old haunts unrecognized. Here, for a day, she felt that she could be herself, not some wife forced into a life and personality that was developed to the expectations of others. As autumn continued to ripen, she knew that she needed to finish her journey home.

By the time she arrived at the family's mansion, her parents were already aware of her resolve to leave her husband and children. Upon reaching her father's estate, she was greeted, not with the love, compassion and affection she had expected, but with anger from her embarrassed parents. In this highly Victorian household, the abandonment of a husband of worth and young children was just not acceptable. Her parents were livid. Humiliated by their high-spirited daughter's choices, a fight ensued even before her luggage reached her room. In the heated exchange that followed, the daughter was ordered from the house and told never to return. In one account, her father actually opened the door and dramatically pointed her out. Displaced and fearful about her future, she spent a restless night in a hotel in Quebec, rather than in the warmth of her father's mansion.

As had become her pattern since leaving England (first, on the boat, then in the hotel in New York City), she responded to the new situation by staying in her room at the hotel. The day after her expulsion, she sat by the window. Through the glass of the window, she watched as some of her childhood friends passed by. This was the second day in just a matter of months when decisions were made that would effect the rest of her life; the first day was when she left her husband and children in England. In Quebec, there were friends and associates upon whom she could have called; these friends could have provided support and guidance. She could have attempted reconciliation by sending an emissary to her parents. Instead of electing a peaceful resolution, she allowed the treatment by her parents, that had manifested itself in anger, to metamorphose into hatred and a desire for vengeance.

As that day rolled on, she decided that she would need a source of funds. From her father and then her husband, she was used to having sufficient resources. Raised to be a lady whose job was to arrange the social aspects of her family's affairs, she had limited skills to offer an employer. Reflecting on her restricted options, she felt it would be best to become a teacher. Her strong will soon prevailed, and she resolved to return to Troy in hopes of obtaining a position as an instructor at the Seminary.

The preceding account may have been well known among those in the inner circle of Troy, but it was not documented anywhere except in Wilson's work.

***

Even today, the number of women who are not married to their true love or who are trapped in an unfulfilling relationship are numerous; but not all women who have left their husbands and children have books written about them. What was it about Mrs. Robinson that resulted in numerous newspaper accounts and two books being written about her (the Wilson book in 1855 and this book in 2004)? She was born to wealth and married into a family with even more money. She was, at the very least, reasonably attractive. It was also true that she had talents and an education well beyond that of most women of her time. Even all of these elements, however, fail to make her worthy of such scrutiny. It was the way she capitalized on these assets that provided the intrigue necessary to hold a reader's interest. Her downfall under the heavy and uneven rules of Victorian Society was not her experiences or her birthright, but rather her choices.

***

Wilson goes on to provide additional information concerning her travel southward from Canada. During this time, those, who could afford to do so, traveled by train or by steamboat. Her return to Troy took a few days. She went first by steamboat up Lake Champlain to the terminus in Whitehall. On this leg of the trip, she noticed a man who would change her life. On the lake boat, she could feel the eyes of a stranger on her whenever she moved. Circumstances being what they were, she assumed that the man was employed either by her father or by her husband to monitor her movements.

In Whitehall, the man who was so consumed by her movements on the trip up the lake introduced himself by presenting his business card. The man was the Commissioner of the Canals, John C. Mather. There were three commissioners, one for each of the three sections; Mather was responsible for the eastern section of the canal. At a time when the canals served as the primary economic thoroughfare for trade between the industrial east and the rural west, Mather was a man of enormous power and even greater political connections. Oddly, Mather's name never appears in Wilson's account.

It is not known how Mrs. Robinson made the final leg of the trip, the section from Whitehall to Troy. Under normal circumstances, the trip would have been made by train. However, having caught the eye of the canal commissioner, she may have traveled the last portion by the more romantic packet boat.

Wilson's account, which is the only report that exists, fails to explain the process by which Mrs. Robinson made the transition from aspiring teacher to mistress. It is evident that she never applied for a position at the Seminary. From other accounts, it is safe to assume that she never even visited her former school. Exactly how soon after her arrival in Troy Mrs. Robinson realized that she could sustain her standard of living by providing a safe haven for men of power is not clear. It is also not clear whether Mather was her first lover or whether he first introduced her to others who could help in her support. What we do know is that by 1851, she had accepted her new life as the mistress of Mather. A little later, she adopted the name Mrs. Robinson.

Her reason for electing to live under the name Mrs. Robinson in Troy is of considerable interest. While she was living in the Capital District, she went by at least two names, the second of which was Mrs. Robinson. In Wilson's interview, Mrs. Robinson told him that the name had a very personal meaning. George III of England was said to have had a mistress named Mrs. Robinson. The first Mrs. Robinson, the King's mistress, bore an illegitimate child while in London; this child's father was George III. The Mrs. Robinson of Troy claimed that she was descended from that child. Having taken on the role of mistress herself, the Mrs. Robinson of Troy, who had married royalty, found herself a kept woman. Having chosen the same relationship as her ancestor, she also chose to use the same name. There is a second explanation for her choice. If Wilson's account is correct, as it probably is, then she had a propensity to return to happy settings. There was, at the time, a family named Robinson who had lived in the area where she lived, probably in the same house. Since the cottage had given her the greatest promise of happiness, she may have adopted its name. The story of being descended from the King's mistress is the far more romantic of the two options.

For almost a year, around 1850, the lady who would be known as Mrs. Robinson, and her French maid, lived in Troy. During this time, she feared being recognized. This problem was exacerbated by her having attended the Seminary, since many of her classmates and men she had met at social functions were still living in the community. Because of the nature of her relationship, she also felt the need to protect Mather. With his political prominence, there was always a concern that some of the people of Troy might see her and put the two together. She was forced to live a sequestered life. She kept to her house, venturing out only under the blanket of darkness. Her French maid did all of the shopping and ran errands during the day. On a rare occasion when she was forced her out in the daytime, she would cover her head and face in a heavy veil.

From a voluntary socialite to a compulsory recluse was not an easy transition. Mrs. Robinson was an extrovert who preferred the company of others to sitting in her apartment. Her life was never satisfactory. As a wife she was in a dismal relationship, but showed that she was capable of fooling all of London into believing that she was happily married. Now she that she was finally in a pleasurable relationship, she had to convince all of Troy that she did not exist.

By 1851 she had convinced her lover to let her move to a residence in a neighboring city. She felt that, in a city where her lover was not as well known, she might be able to live a more open life. Such may have been the case, but not when the city chosen was the State capital. Albany was chosen, probably because it was the only community of significant size. Whoever, Mrs. Robinson or Mather, chose Albany did not understand the politics of a state capital. Capitals, by their very nature, are consumed by intrigue. Capitals are built and sustained on speculation. Whether the intrigue is social, political, economic, or criminal makes little difference; the people are taught to feed on knowledge that they believe is shared by only a few. In an environment like Albany, the existence of a sanctuary where the Canal Commissioner could stop to spend a few relaxing hours could hardly be overlooked for long.

In Albany, the neighbors began to gossip about Mather and his mistress. They knew who he was, but the identity of the woman he visited was much harder to ascertain. She appeared to have true social graces, hardly what was considered the norm for women of her talent. The lack of factual knowledge only raised the desire to be the first to find out the specifics about her. When people cannot prove a fact, speculation increases. As speculation increases, so does the desire to know the essentials. Thus begins a rumor frenzy that can only be stemmed by the proof of some aspect of the question. The very fact that Mrs. Robinson was so successful at hiding her real identity only heightened the interest of her neighbors.

Probably because she was trying to hide so much, if there was one thing that Mrs. Robinson despised, it was the belief that people were talking about her. The fact that her neighbors in Albany were discussing her could hardly be missed. For some unexplained reason, Mrs. Robinson ascribed the root of all the rumors to one Irish maid whom she believed practiced witchcraft. According to her lover's interview with Wilson, she took it upon herself to buy a revolver to use against the maid. The maid, hearing of Mrs. Robinson's plot, swore out a warrant for her arrest.

One evening, while Mrs. Robinson and Mather were sitting at dinner, there was a knock on the door. It was an Albany police officer serving the warrant issued for the maid. It was obvious that Wilson was quoting Mather as he told of the lover boldly accompanying her to police court. After hearing the charges and entering a preliminary plea of "not guilty," Mather paid her bail. The issue was not pressed any further.

After the arrest, the neighborhood in Albany no longer met the needs of the two lovers. Mrs. Robinson decided it would be better to move to a quieter part of Albany. Albany being Albany, the rumors of her behavior arrived at her new home before she did. Again her neighbors were talking about the unknown lady.

It was soon evident that there was no social benefit to the move across Albany, so the two lovers resigned themselves to returning to Troy. It would also be more convenient for Mather to join her for quick visits in Troy. In the spring of 1852 the perfect cottage was found. It sat well back from the road. A large brick house blocked the exposure of the cottage from the south; on the other side was a mill. The cottage had pillars and a front porch. The river to the back prevented unwanted eyes from spying on the couple from that direction. The place was gracious yet humble, a mix that was hard to find. It was also far enough from the center of Troy for Mather to visit with fewer prying eyes becoming aware.

The depth of the relationship that Mrs. Robinson shared with Mather is difficult to measure. One thing they both acknowledged was that their companionship had to be kept secret. He had become her only link to the social world that she so sadly missed. It was true that in the cottage she had a maid and a gardener to attend to her and to the needs of the house, but they were only servants. She had been raised to treat people according to their station. They were loyal, and she was loyal in return, but they could never be her confidants; after all, they were not her equals.

The standards of the Victorian Era were not as simple as they are often portrayed. All members of society were expected to act in public according to a strict social code which repressed sexuality and supported charity. Yet it was a time when avarice and prostitution were more blatant and prevalent. Successful businessmen were expected to have a wife and a family. Their children were to go to the best schools, and their wives were to join in benefits and plan the family's social calendar. Society was wearing a mask. Many, perhaps most, successful businessmen kept an apartment in town where they would house a companion. The only true mistake was in being found out, usually resulting in a scandal.

Like today, the middle class struggled to live within society's values. The rich and poor, then as now, were in a position to do what felt good. Those on the perimeter of society take from life whatever pleasures they can find; the only difference money provides is the setting where the amusements happen and the quality of the food and drink.

Whenever Mather came by, Mrs. Robinson hung on his every word. For those who were offended by their relationship or were by nature callous, her loyalty would be considered bought, paid for by the man who regularly deposited into her bank account. In reality, her attention was much more. Not only did she live off Mather, she also lived through him. Her only victories were the ones he attained. Her losses were both her own and any disappointments he experienced. She was his confidant, his devoted supporter. When he was with her, he enjoyed her undivided attention. Their union grew stronger in times of peril, and political peril was about to come down on him. Their candy jar of happiness was about to be set upon by the malicious side of politics. In the spring of 1853, John C. Mather was in trouble.

As 1853 approached, Mrs. Robinson became even more pensive and moody. For over two years, she had lived in the shadows of society. She missed the theater, parties, the general activities that had meant so much to her before she returned to America. Quietly, and without providing any indications to Mather, Mrs. Robinson made plans to return to England, her husband and children. She was not sure that he would take her back, but better to have tried a dream and failed than to have spent a lifetime watching a dream pass. It was a gamble that she felt was worth the risk.

When Mather was out of town on business, Mrs. Robinson took a train to Boston from which she planned to board a ship before he returned. She did everything she could to cover her escape. She had not used the name Mrs. Robinson when she purchased the train ticket. In Boston she stayed at the Revere House while she waited for the ship on which she had booked passage. When Mather returned to Troy earlier than expected, he went to visit her at the cottage. Learning from the maid that she was not home, he intimidated the poor servant into telling him where Mrs. Robinson had gone. The cast off lover boarded the next train to Boston, in pursuit of his consort.

Arriving in Boston, he went immediately to the hotel where he obtained her room number. When she answered the door, she was startled to see him. They talked as lovers do when having a spat. There were tears; there were the promises lovers make when devotion has been shown. Eventually, she rescinded her promise to leave and agreed to return to their life in Troy. They arrived back at the cottage the next day.

The story of her flight and his pursuit provides insight into the depth of the feelings of each. She was lonely and willing to humble herself in front of her husband. On Mather's part it shows that, either he knew that she was having problems and was willing to deal with them, or she did not really have the problems that he told to Wilson. In any event, this would have been the perfect opportunity for Mather to be rid of her. To the contrary, he showed his devotion by pursuing her to Boston.

There is one other very important behavior that Wilson's stories indicate. Whenever Mrs. Robinson felt that the pressure was too much, she fled. She left her husband and children in London rather than stay and work to improve the situation; she fled Quebec after the confrontation with her parents. She fled Troy for the possibility of safety and security in London. In each case she was not sure what her reception would be, but she would take the risk rather than stay and deal with the stress. Why then did she not flee when she knew she was under investigation for the poisoning of Timothy Lanagan and Catherine Lubbee? What she did that evening was to go shopping. Is this change in behavior an indication that she was innocent, or is it further proof that she was insane?

Her Lover

The man whose name everyone feared to say aloud, but rejoiced in whispering –

The man who visited Mrs. Robinson only in the dark of night –

The man who paid her bills and provided her with a maid and gardener –

The man whose power nearly exceeded his new wealth –

The man whose name was never printed in the newspapers, even after the murders, was Canal Commissioner John C. Mather, one of the most powerful men in New York State government. This was a time when New York deserved its nickname, the Empire State, and the main reason for this status was the Erie Canal. The Erie Canal was to commerce what the internet is to communication. To be in charge of the eastern third of the canal, like Mather, was to be responsible for the largest single source of revenue for the State government.

To gain a perspective on Mather and his heritage, one only needs to learn what his middle initial, C., stood for; his full name was John Cotton Mather. He was a direct descendant of Cotton Mather, the fiery minister who presided over the Salem Witch Trials. Although one cannot choose his relatives, one's upbringing can be anticipated by the names their parents select. It is obvious that Mather's father, a doctor, first in Deposit and then in Binghamton, New York, was proud of his passionate ancestor. Men who hold religious figures in such high esteem almost certainly raise their children under narrowly delineated rules. Because of these standards, John Mather could see little that was gray; to him, all things were clearer if they were in either black or white.

Mather had two brothers; one was a professor at, what is now, the University of Massachusetts. His other brother, Cullen Mather, was an attorney who started out in Troy, but, by the time of the incident with Mrs. Robinson, had moved his practice to New York City.

John C. Mather found the metropolis of Troy more to his liking than his native Deposit and relocated to Troy in his early twenties, entering into the manufacturing and warehouse businesses. Financially, he was very successful. Politically, he was equally successful, starting his political career as an alderman in his adopted city. He was appointed Loan Commissioner by two different governors. In 1847, he ran for the position of Canal Commissioner but was defeated, along with the entire Democratic ticket. During that election, there was a split in the party, and one faction known as the "Barnburners" boycotted the polls. Despite his loss in the election, Mather received considerable notice, as he drew more votes than anyone else on the ticket. By 1850, the Democrats had temporarily learned their lesson and ran a ticket that represented both factions of the party. This time, Mather was elected to a three-year term as Canal Commissioner.

The Erie Canal was more than twenty-five years old and in need of improvements. Shortly after Mather became commissioner, the state established a fund, known as the Seven Million Dollar Bill, to make the necessary modifications. The disbursement of these funds would generate an attack on Mather. In fairness, it may have been a desire to diminish his rapidly-growing power that made the opposing party set out to embarrass him.

Politics Unusual

The story of Mrs. Robinson and John C. Mather cannot be fully understood unless it is examined within the context of the social and political agenda of the era. The period between the elections of 1844 and 1868 was a tumultuous period for America's political structure. The issues of westward expansion, the rapid increase in immigration, and slavery constantly lurked just below the surface of the national agenda. Positions on these issues either split or unified families, neighbors and political parties.

Prior to 1860, the speed of the railroads had made it relatively convenient for wealthy southern plantation owners to leave the oppressive heat of the south and to vacation in Saratoga and the other spas in the northeast for the summer season. By 1830 all of the northern states had abolished slavery. The southern families brought their household slaves with them as they visited the free north. The differences between the cultures were not something that people just heard about; they were something that they witnessed first hand each year.

At the beginning of this period, there were, primarily, two political parties: the Democrats and the Whigs; at the end of the period, there were still two political parties: the Democrats and the Republicans. The shift was not so simple as a mere change in the name of the Whig Party. In fact most of the people who became Republicans started out as Democrats. The major catalyst for the reorganization was the Compromise of 1850, which allowed the expansion of slavery into parts of what was then called the western territories. The Republicans, who would soon be headed by Abraham Lincoln, opposed the expansion of slavery, and supported small business. The Democrats supported farmers, a distinction that plantation owners in the south used to describe themselves. The reality was that plantation owners were businessmen who made their livings from agriculture, not people who did the everyday work. As a party, the Democrats did not oppose slavery. The relationships among politicians over these issues were so strong that they did not consider themselves as opponents so much as enemies.

The trial of Mrs. Robinson did not happen amid the political divisions of the day, but more as a result of them. She became a pawn, caught in the middle of forces that, in order to gain their own victories, would step on the rights and lives of individuals who were inconvenient. John C. Mather was elected canal commissioner as a Democrat; by the time this period was over, Mather would be a

Tammany Hall Democrat in New York City.

The two teams of lawyers who were lined up in this trial did so directly along party lines. The prosecution lawyers were soft Democrats, aligning themselves with former President Van Buren. The defense lawyers were hard Democrats aligning themselves with William Seward. Judge Harris was a Whig. When the trial was over, the prosecution lawyer, Judge Harris, and Martin Townsend would all be Republicans. The remainder of the defense team and Mather would remain Democrats.

To understand the politics of the trial, we need to examine Thurlow Weed, the editor of the *Albany Express* newspaper. During this time, newspapers were politically active, and editors used their pages to promote their own agendas. Weed was such a champion; in this arena he was known among the politically astute as the "Little Dictator." Weed was the driving force behind the Whig Party, and, according to some, one of the major reasons for the party's demise. In 1848, Weed was one of the major supporters of the Zachary Taylor / Millard Filmore ticket. Like Weed, Taylor had opposed the Compromise of 1850; both men believed that slavery should not be allowed to expand into the western territories. When Taylor died unexpectedly, the virtually unknown Filmore was suddenly thrust into leading the country through these divisive times. In an effort to keep the country from a civil war, Filmore backed the Compromise. Unable to get Filmore to change his perception, Weed abandoned him and left him to serve out his term ineffectively. This process of abandoning those who were inconvenient became a trademark of both Weed and the Whigs. Simply put, you had to either support Weed's position on any issue, or you had to deal with him as your enemy. It will be shown later that this hard-nosed practice actually served Harris. Although John C. Mather was not in the same party as Weed, he watched the wily old politician with the eye one uses for a sage.

Thurlow Weed

Another example of Weed's power, and the way that he used it, is shown by its impact on the events of this story. One of Weed's weaker political moments was the New York statewide election in 1850. As noted previously, he had lost on the national issue of the Compromise. To further diminish his power, his party's slate lost the 1850 state election to the Democratic Party. In the spring of 1853, Weed thought that he had been given an opportunity to even the score. His Whigs, in combination with the soft Democrats, began to examine Mather and his use of the money intended to improve the Canal. Eventually, this group thought that they had enough information to embarrass Mather and the Democrats by holding an impeachment trial. In June of 1853, less than a month after the murders of Lanagan and Lubbee, the state Legislature met to settle the question of impeachment. When it came time for a roll call vote, Weed's supporters, realizing that they were not in the majority, decided not to support the impeachment. Unexpectedly, the Democrats, and Mather's allies voted for impeachment. They were going to use the process to publicly exonerate Mather. Weed was caught off guard; he had intended to embarrass his enemy. Now he was once again the man who had to regroup.

Mather was charged with ten counts of mismanagement of funds. Since Mather was the first person ever impeached in New York State, when the charges were filed, no one even knew the process for holding an impeachment trial. The press had a great time. Weed's opponents relished making him look bad. They covered the trial until it was so obvious that Mather was innocent that people stopped following the case. In September of 1853, Mather was acquitted on all counts.

Mather treated his mistress, Mrs. Robinson, following Weed's practice of abandonment (Filmore); he also followed the Democrats' custom of defending with the best lawyers (her trial). The difference was that Mather was not Weed; although Mather was good, he was not great at the behind-the-scenes tricks, like Weed.

Another difference is that one can sting his enemy once, but the second time becomes far more difficult. In this situation, Mrs. Robinson's trial came after the Mather Trial, and the soft Democrats and Whigs had positioned themselves much better than they had in the Mather trial. Weed was not going to go down without a fight, even if the fight was not the one he would have chosen.

Mather had been married and later separated from his wife. The separation occurred at nearly the same time that he became involved with Mrs. Robinson. Since there was no date ever given as to the beginning of their relationship, it is not clear if the split in Mather's marriage was caused by his relationship with Henrietta. The census of 1850 shows that he was then living in a boarding house. This census shows one other interesting fact; Mather had already begun to lie about his age. At the time of the census he was 37; he reported that he was 35. As time went on, he would continue to shave years off his actual age.

In Jail

As time went on, it was discovered that the mysterious Mrs. Robinson was many things, and blamed for being even more. One thing of which she was never accused was being a model prisoner.

On the night of her arrest, Mrs. Robinson had changed into her night gown before the coroner, Reed Bontecou, arrived at about 9:00 p.m. The gown she put on was considered short, meaning that it probably came to her ankles. Bontecou told her he was a doctor and that it was his responsibility to search her person. Before he began his physical search, Bontecou was struck by her appearance, especially her eyes. People who saw her that night were all taken by the wild appearance of her eyes. Although it was not a part of his general practice to assess a person's sanity, Bontecou could not help feeling that she was irrational in her behavior.

The first night, as the shock of the arrest and the understanding of her whereabouts settled in, she began raving. The jailor who was in charge that night could hear her calling out for the police. He became concerned that she might be suicidal and stationed himself at a point from which he could monitor her cell without being seen. For hours she continued to call out for help. It was as if the men who were harassing her, so much that she had gone to see Brownell, were outside her cell. She ranted on for the entire night.

One of the more interesting situations involving the detention of Mrs. Robinson dealt with her possessions. Within the first two days following her arrest, Mrs. Robinson was taken from the cell usually reserved for the female prisoners and shown the top floor of the jail. She was asked if she might not prefer the comfort of this entire floor to sharing the floors below. Her options were to literally have her own apartment or to be among those who found themselves housed in the jail for the night or longer. She chose the top floor of the jail.

Bontecou returned to the jail on the day following the search of her cottage to ask Mrs. Robinson what she wanted done about her furniture. Again Bontecou was fixated by her behavior. It was not so much her gestures that made him wonder; it was still something in her eyes. There was a wildness about her gaze. She was sitting in the one chair in her cell, and, when he asked her questions, she did not answer, but just continued to talk about whatever was on her mind. After approximately fifteen minutes of unresponsive behavior, Bontecou gave up and left the room. As Bontecou was leaving, he watched her walk to the window. His last memory of her that day was of her silhouette as she just stared out at the city that had transitioned in a brief time from her adopted home and sanctuary into a place set on her downfall.

Over the next fortnight, Bontecou saw her on an average of three times per week. Ostensibly, his visits were to ask her about the dispensation of her possessions. After each visit, he left with the impression that she was not rational. Frustrated, he decided to test her for himself. One time he told her that he heard that Lubbee and Lanagan were dead. Bontecou thought about her reaction and realized that, if she did understand his words, there was no appearance of it through any action or reaction. She had not even seemed to notice his words. The last week he visited her, he decided to push her and ask the question straight out. He said, "You know they say you have poisoned those people, and I want you to tell me about it.": after a short pause he continued, "All about it." Mrs. Robinson just continued to talk about the same old "jumble" she had been talking about when he asked her the question.

One day when Bontecou came to the cell to check on the disposal of Mrs. Robinson's property, he told her that he had been asked by Mrs. Lanagan to please return a pot, a strainer, and a bonnet. Bontecou went on to clarify to Mrs. Robinson that

Mrs. Lanagan had told him that these objects belonged to her. After his explanation, Bontecou asked Mrs. Robinson directly if it was all right to return the items; she barely looked up, responding, "Why not?"

Over the course of the next two weeks, Bontecou sent most of Mrs. Robinson's clothes to the jail. After her cell was changed on the second day, she had much more room. Most of her furniture was also taken to the jail, where she set up housekeeping in, what became, her own apartment. When Bontecou finally handed over the key to the cottage to Dr. Hegemen, the doctor/jailer, he stopped visiting Mrs. Robinson.

***

By the standards of that day, the year between Mrs. Robinson's arrest and her trial was considered to be a very long time. In the 1850's, justice was swift, with virtually all trials held within one to six months of the arrest. During the year that she languished in jail, there was considerable speculation about Mrs. Robinson's sanity. There was also a rumor about her identity that ran rampant throughout the community. More importantly, there were a number of developments and incidents involving Mrs. Robinson and some of the other principal characters in this story.

The question of a person's sanity was even less well understood in the Victorian Era than it is today. Definitions aside, the critical difference was in the treatment of people with mental problems. Today many people are able to handle mental issues through the use of various drugs. In Mrs. Robinson's time, if the family could not keep the person at home, the person was usually placed in a lunatic asylum. In many ways, these asylums served as warehouses for people unable to function in society. Even in the best asylums, there was little or no treatment provided. Some, with less serious cases of mental illness, were kept in the County Home in which the people were expected to work to offset the expense of their housing; these were the lucky ones.

Mrs. Robinson was an intelligent woman who would have known her fate had she been found insane. As bad as prison may have appeared, the thought of life in an asylum would have appeared much worse. For the entire year, she consistently resisted the label of insanity. The community, however, was only too willing to pass judgment on the issue. Although there was no official poll, it appears the line was not in the center; most people felt that she was feigning insanity in an effort to escape punishment, this despite the fact that no one could figure out her motive for the murders.

Throughout Troy, during the summer of 1853, there was considerable speculation as to the identity of Mrs. Robinson. Although no one could directly cite the source of the information, it was widely held that her real name was Emma Wood, of the prominent Wood family of Quebec.

The rumor that Mrs. Robinson was one of the Wood sisters began immediately upon her arrest. Robert Wood, of Quebec, was a very successful merchant and trader. By the standards of the day, the Wood family was considered to be immensely wealthy. The mid-nineteenth century was the first era during which members of the middle class were wealthier than some nobility. Often, to support their lifestyle, members of the nobility married members of the wealthy middle class. The middle class had its first opportunity to become nobility through marriage. These inter-class marriages were a symbiotic relationship. Wood's wealth was indicated by the fact that four of his five daughters married into British nobility.

The excellent reputation of the Seminary in Troy is demonstrated by the fact that, regardless of whether Mrs. Robinson was Emma Wood or not, four of the five Wood sisters did attend the Women's Seminary at Troy. It was a place for wealthy families to send their daughters to be educated and to be safe.

The Troy community at large believed, based on trinkets of information, that Mrs. Robinson let out during the period from March to May, that her real name was Emma Wood. It was also understood that several of the sons of professional men in Troy had attended the socials held at the seminary. These men were reported to have seen her in Troy either before her arrest or subsequent to it, and they all agreed that Mrs. Robinson was one of the Wood sisters. This belief was supported through the alleged identification of her by the son of one of her lawyers (based on his age, this would have been one of Beach's sons).

The problem with this rumor is that not many people were actually able to see Mrs. Robinson while she was incarcerated. It is true that, during the entire time she was incarcerated, people would drop by the jail to see the notorious woman. In her opinion, she had become a sideshow feature. A practice was set up that, in order to see Mrs. Robinson, a person had to be involved in the case or given permission by her. True to her nature, she refused to see anyone, which means that her only visitors were people involved in the case. A second point that discredits the rumor of her recognition needs to be stressed. After a couple of days, no one, not even her attorneys, got to see her without her veil. The only exceptions to her shroud of mystery were the Sheriff, his family and the deputies.

The belief that she was one of the Wood sisters was supported by a second unsubstantiated rumor that was circulating. Accord to the gossip mill, in the middle of June, a man from Canada suddenly appeared in Troy. It was widely held that this man was a representative of Mrs. Robinson's brother, William. It was known that this stranger, unlike almost everyone else, had been allowed to visit her in her cell. What is not certain, but easy to believe, is that she had promised during that visit never to reveal her true identity. What is known is that, after the stranger left, she always had plenty of money to pay for any necessities she might want while in jail.

What is less certain is the explanation for all of the most able attorneys in Troy being on her defense team. The attorneys may have been engaged by the stranger, but it is far more likely that they were assembled by Mrs. Robinson's lover.

***

In July of 1853, a mysterious item appeared in the newspapers. The note was from Mr. Willard, the head of the Seminary. Through publishing this note, it was Willard's desire to set aside the rumor that Mrs. Robinson was a member of the Wood family. Willard noted that he had been assured by William Wood that all of his sisters were living in England. In Willard's note he said that, if Mrs. Robinson were a graduate of the school, she would most certainly have visited the Seminary while she was in town. Willard also said that William Wood, the supposed brother, had recently visited Troy and had met for over an hour with the woman who claimed to be Emma Wood. Mr. Willard stated that Mr. Wood was certain that the woman in the Troy jail was not one of his sisters.

There are four important questions raised by Mr. Willard's note. First, if Mr. Wood was sure that all of his sisters were all in

England, why would he have traveled all the way from Quebec to visit with a stranger? Second, why did Mr. Willard assume that a woman who was trying to hide her identity and who was living the life of a mistress, would visit her alma mater? Third, why would a successful professional man like Mr. Wood spend an hour with a woman who was not his sister? The questions raised by the length of the visit are compounded by the consideration that Mrs. Robinson was insane.

There is one even more important point than those questions. Mr. Willard implied in his note that the woman arrested as Mrs. Robinson was claiming to be one of the Wood sisters. This is a blatant misrepresentation. There is no evidence anywhere that she ever gave any indication of her real identity before her trial. She would not share her past, even with her own lawyers. This woman was consistently veiled for a reason. Unlike the projection made by Willard, this was a lady who wanted no one to find out her real identity.

***

There was another doctor who visited Mrs. Robinson much more often than Dr. Bontecou. The second doctor's name was William Hegemen. Hegemen epitomizes the term versatile. There is a line that you can tell a small town because each business does more than one type of business (i.e. the knitting store takes dry cleaning). Hegemen was a small town physician in a city. In addition to being a doctor, Hegemen was one of Price's deputies. He was a man who could confine you to a cell or bed, whichever was appropriate. To add to Hegemen's knowledge of the defendant, he resided in a room at the jail. Hegemen soon acquired the habit of visiting Mrs. Robinson three or more times each day. This practice was fairly consistent from a few days after the arrest until the time of the trial.

On the night of her arrest, Hegemen only saw Mrs. Robinson for a moment as she went up the stairs. It was on the second day that he actually met her for the first time. He was immediately drawn by her eyes and her dress. On that occasion, Hegemen noted that her eyes seemed to have an "unnatural appearance," so much so that he used the same term for her eyes as Bontecou, "wild." Being used to women prisoners, almost all of whom were arrested at that time for vagrancy, intoxication, or being a harlot, Mrs. Robinson's dirty clothing did not look out of place. Hegemen would soon learn that she was, on other occasions, a very well-dressed woman. On the first morning after her arrest, her dress was hanging loosely about her body and was dirty. Hegemen noted that her demeanor was "irritable and sullen." Hegemen, as one of her guards, noted that she spent most of the first full day sitting in the lone chair in her cell, but when she walked, it was in very quick movements.

On the first morning when Hegemen went to her cell, Mrs. Robinson told him that she had heard Oliver Boutwell's men gathering in the cells next to hers. She told Hegemen that she could hear the men sharpening their knives all night, because they were out to "destroy" her. Hegemen tried to tell her that the cells on both sides of her were empty and dark. She told Hegemen that she knew better and demanded that he return her pistols so that she might defend herself. Naturally, he refused. She insisted a second time, saying that she needed the guns to protect herself from the ruffians. Hegemen said that, if the need arose, he would be there to protect her. Mrs. Robinson would not listen to what she considered to be his flimsy explanations, claiming that the men were already in the jail and, that he was covering for them.

As he tried to leave the cell she was in, Mrs. Robinson grabbed him and held on. He would later say that the only way he was able to get out of the cell was to "disengage myself by force."

It was Hegemen who suggested that she move into the bigger cell, the one on the top floor, the one she occupied for the rest of the time. Hegemen was also the person who made the final arrangements to have her clothes and furniture moved to the jail. Her furniture, as it turned out, was the envy of many. Among her possessions while she was in jail consisted of at least a bed, wardrobe, washstand, divan, several tables, six chairs, mirrors, dishes, and a rocking chair.

Mrs. Robinson had three other visitors the first morning. She was visited by one of her future attorneys, Job Pierson. Two other young attorneys, Storer and Richard C. Jennyss, also came to her cell. While Pierson would claim that he was there to represent Mrs. Robinson's interests, the other two were there to represent the interests of her lover. While Pierson was there to protect Mrs. Robinson, Storer and R. C. Jennyss were at the jail to get some letters that her lover had written.

Hegemen later remembered that, on the second night that she was in the jail, she screamed so forcefully that he stayed up all night to watch her. He was sure she was going to "destroy" herself that night. He noted that she was certain that a mob was outside the jail. In fact, there was no one outside. Throughout the night Mrs. Robinson kept calling out for the police to protect her.

The morning after the "night of the mob," Jennyss visited Mrs. Robinson for the second time. She was consumed by a fear for her own safety. She told Jennyss that on the previous evening a group of two to three hundred had broken into the jail. According to Mrs. Robinson, the mob got all the way to her cell before Sheriff Price was able to stop them. As if this were not enough of a tale of woe, she went on to say that even after Price got the mob out of the jail, she was still almost killed by a couple who were already in the jail. She told him that a man and woman from uptown (the area where she lived) had arranged to be arrested just so they could be in the jail to kill her. She told Jennyss that during the night they had filled a cauldron with water and heated it until it was boiling. The couple then broke into her cell and started to abuse her. Ultimately, they told her to "either get in the pot or they would put me in." She said, "I know I have got to die." She then tried to negotiate, saying that, if the couple would stop abusing her, she would get into the pot. She told Jennyss that the noise was loud enough that others came to the cell. The couple, when they heard the others coming, ran off. As she finished the story, she ran her hands along the sides of her dress and asked Jennyss, "Don't I look shabby?" Then she began to laugh. Through out this entire visit, Jennyss could not help noticing that her eyes were distorted and dilated.

For the first two weeks – about the same time that Dr. Bontecou was visiting – Hegemen was unable to engage Mrs. Robinson in a coherent conversation. As a result of her inco-herent behavior, he was able to clearly remember her response when he told her one day that the funeral procession for Lanagan and Lubbee was passing by the jail. Hegemen said something to the effect that the sounds were from the funeral for the two people she was supposed to have murdered. Mrs. Robinson merely replied, "It is queer, isn't it." She then began laughing and went back to talking about another subject.

Without being asked to do an assessment of her mental condition, Hegeman had undertaken an examination for his "own mind." As a physician was his judgment, although not hers, was that she was not of sound mind. He felt that her mental condition for the entire time she was incarcerated was unsound, but that it slightly improved before her trial. Hegemen was made very much aware of her condition when she broke up her fine furniture and burned it in the wood stove. The outbursts during which she burned the furniture almost always occurred when she heard news about her upcoming trial. Over the course of the year, she broke up five of the six chairs in her cell. She also broke up the desk and part of the couch.

When Hegemen took over the case, he was careful to be sure that she had no alcohol. To his knowledge, the only drinks she had been allowed during the entire year between the arrest and the trial were brandy and wine that he ordered for medicinal purposes the previous autumn.

Another Poisoning

On Monday July 21, 1853, *The Troy Whig* carried a caustic article pertaining to an episode involving Mrs. Robinson. The *Whig* reported that, on the previous Saturday, Mrs. Robinson had attempted to kill herself by deliberately taking a mineral poison. The newspaper depicted the incident as providing one more example of how self-administered poison added another "feature to the already revolting character" of the events in the story of the dual poisoning. The article had a sarcastic tone, which probably reflected the feelings of many of the newspaper's readers. It was now eight weeks into the story, and most of Troy was immersed in the events surrounding the Robinson case and reports relating to her identity. The regional newspapers were carrying some information, but, to a large extent, the people were starving for more information concerning anyone who was involved. As is often the case, when there were no new facts coming out, the people filled in the holes with rumors.

The day after the *Whig* article appeared, *The Troy Times* carried a critique which also presented a mocking attitude toward the poison at the jail. The *Times* went even further in its assault, implying that Mrs. Robinson had a propensity toward the use of poison to solve her problems.

In his report of the incident, Sheriff Price stated that he had visited Henrietta's cell at noon. At that time, he brought her the dinner that his wife had prepared. Upon arriving at her cell, the sheriff noticed Mrs. Robinson was lying quietly on her bed. She was so still that she appeared to the sheriff to be asleep. Assuming she was merely taking a nap, he chose not to wake her and left the meal in the cell for her to eat when she awoke. According to Price, in a bragging tone, he noted that he was careful not to disturb her sleep, slipping quietly out of her space in the jail. At 4:00 that afternoon, one of the attendants (not one of the deputies) of the jail went on rounds; on his cycle, he checked on the condition of Mrs. Robinson. This person had checked on Mrs. Robinson previously that day. On the second trip he noticed that she was still lying down but by now had vomited several times; the contents of her stomach had a bluish color. The attendant immediately sought the sheriff.

When Price got into her cell, he asked the groggy Henrietta what had occurred. She said that she had taken "a considerable quantity of vitriol (a word meaning anger)." According to the sheriff, Mrs. Robinson went on to say that she had taken enough "to end her life." The sheriff said that Mrs. Robinson elaborated saying that it was "okay" since she was, "heartily tired of life." In his statement, the sheriff said that she had remarked that she had seen "trouble enough."

At the direction of Price, two doctors were called to provide medical assistance. Ironically, one of the doctors summoned was Dr. Adams, the same physician who had been unsuccessful in treating Timothy Lanagan. True to the code of their profession and not being judgmental, the doctors administered what they believed were the appropriate antidotes. There were those in the city who might have been content if the doctors had done nothing. That night there was a question as to whether she would recuperate; by Sunday morning she was weak, but on her way to recovery.

The question was raised as to how she had gotten a foreign

substance into her cell. The assumption, given by the *Whig*, was that she had it on her person when she initially entered the cell weeks before "carefully concealed in some portion of her superabundant wardrobe." The *Times* was less concerned about how she obtained the poison, than for what purpose it was procured. They wondered why she would want to take her own life. One option for how she could have acquired the substance was brought out at her trial. Several of the witnesses who visited her in jail during the period between her arrest and this incident were questioned as to whether they had brought anything, which today we would consider contraband, into her cell on their visitations. They all answered in the negative. Although it was not advocated during the Victorian Era, bringing things to a person in jail was much less of a concern, than it is today.

There are at least three possible scenarios for what transpired in Mrs. Robinson's cell that Saturday. The first and most obvious explanation is that Mrs. Robinson attempted suicide. The second possibility is that she may also have had the substance put in her food by someone else, just as happened to Lanagan and Lubbee. With the impeachment charges filed against Mather, it was clear that Mrs. Robinson had evolved into an inconvenient woman. Said in polite terms, she had become an embarrassment to Mather, his friends and to the city of Troy. Having her story end in her cell on a hot summer afternoon would have served the needs of, not one, but many, people. Attempted murder is an easy hypothesis to accept.

Even Robinson's own words leave open the possibility that she was poisoned by someone else. She was quoted as saying that she had taken vitriol, but did not say that it was by her own hand. Even the expression that she had taken enough "to end her life" does not mean that it was deliberate; it could just be a reaction to the pain she was suffering and the self-assurance of her imminent death. The real doubt about self-administration comes into question with her statement that it was "okay". If she thought it was administered by another, she might well have said it was "okay" as a way of expressing forgiveness for whoever had poisoned her. Saying that she was, "heartily tired of life," and that she had seen "trouble enough," might imply suicide or might be an expression of acceptance.

There was a third, much simpler, and far more plausible explanation than any of those presented at the time. In the 1850's, prisoners in local jails were treated very dissimilarly to today. In fact they were treated very differently even from each other. Prisoners, if they had funds, were allowed to have their personal furniture, clothes, and jewelry in their cells. It was even possible for prisoners in the jail to have their meals prepared outside, by restaurants, and brought to their cells. It was a "perk" of the position of jailer to be given tips for providing items including alcohol, medicines and favors. An explanation for what happened to Mrs. Robinson might well be found in the implementation of the favors process.

As mentioned previously, *The Troy Times* carried a sarcastic article on the day following the story in the *Whig*. There was a major contrast in the amount of news each carried by of the newspapers. The *Times* carried much more news in general than the *Whig*. The *Whig,* at this time, was mostly advertisements and opinions. Another article appeared in the *Times* on the same day that it reported that Mrs. Robinson had taken the poison. The second article was relegated to a far less prominent position in the paper, over one column and down to the left of the story about Mrs. Robinson. The second article told of two young boys who had been accidentally poisoned on the previous Saturday. It seems the boys had developed summer coughs; in an effort to relieve their congestion, and to help the boys get a good night's rest, their mother had gone to the local druggist and asked for lanthanum. An investigation into the incident with the boys found that the young clerk had mixed up two drugs and had actually given the mother a poison by mistake. It needs to be noted that the drugstore in question was only one block from the jail. If Mrs. Robinson had sent one of the jailers in search of a "remedy" to relieve her anxiety, he would most likely have gone to that same store. The remedy would almost certainly have been lanthanum. There is a very real likelihood that the clerk made the same mistake twice in the same day.

Having ingested what she thought was going to ease her pains, Mrs. Robinson found that instead, she was very ill and facing death. It is possible that Mrs. Robinson uttered the quotes repeated by Sheriff Price, not because she intended to end her own life, but because of the pain and irony of the whole situation.

Hegemen was away from the jail when the poisoning incident took place. The fact that Hegemen was not present provides more credence to the possibility that either someone had snuck something into Mrs. Robinson's drink, or that she had sent a jailer to the drugstore to get her lanthanum.

Over the course of the year, Hegemen realized that Mrs. Robinson did not like the idea of being considered insane. She would resist any suggestion of insanity. What she told Hegemen as the trial approached was, "I am not insane now." She failed to tell him the date she had recovered.

On October 10, 1853, a Grand Jury arraigned Mrs. Robinson on two charges of murder in the first degree. At the arraignment, she pleaded "not guilty"; she also provided a preview of some of the behaviors that would become associated with her name. That day she wore a black dress that had a low neckline, an elegant lace collar and lace cuffs on the sleeves; she was also heavily adorned with jewelry. He outfit was estimated to have cost between two and three hundred dollars. This was at a time when the average family lived on less than $300 a year. She was wearing one year's income for her neighbors. The last item that she wore was the one for which she would become famous. She wore a heavy, dark blue veil that prevented anyone from seeing her face.

At the arraignment, more evidence emerged regarding Mrs. Robinson's mental state. The judge wanted to set a date for the trial; he started by suggesting that the trial begin before November. The defense asked that the trial be postponed; Martin Townsend, a second attorney obtained for Mrs. Robinson's defense, told the judge that it was only recently that his client was in any condition to help in her own defense. The judge granted the stay. More importantly, the lawyer's statement acknowledges that by mid-October Mrs. Robinson was acting more rationally.

In February the question of a trial date again came before the judge. By this time, the prosecution knew the skill level of the defense. District Attorney Anson Bingham hired an attorney from out of the county, Henry Hogeboom, to assist in the prosecution of the case. In reviewing the indictment, Hogeboom had discovered some irregularities which he felt might be used by the defense to negate the outcome of the trial, if Mrs. Robinson were convicted. Hogeboom asked for a stay so that a new bill of charges could be drafted. The judge acceded to his request.

Mrs. Robinson was hardly a placid prisoner. Over the course of the winter, she broke up and burned several pieces of her furniture. The furniture was burned in the woodstove that was used to heat her cell. The breaking of the furniture was probably not necessary since the guards were supplying her with the normal ration of firewood, and she could have purchased more wood from the guards. There were two explanations for her behavior. To some it was evidence that she was not warm enough and wanted more heat. The second was that it was done in anger, since each instance of breaking furniture coincided with an event in the court system – usually a postponement.

By April, the gap between the murders and the trial was becoming exceeding long (ten months). The *Troy Times* said that this gap did nothing to provide a resolution for the people of Troy, but only supported the idea that there were people who, for political reasons, were trying to prevent the trial from ever happening. The *Times* assured its readers that, "If this trial is again put over, we shall endeavor to learn the true reasons." The newspaper went on to complain about the cost to taxpayers of keeping her in jail. In one of the first signs of the yellow journalism that was to become more prevalent in a few years, the *Times* went on: "If there is to be more trifling with justice in this matter, the people demand to know why it is, and we shall endeavor to give them the reason, if any can be found." It was more of a threat than a reality. At this time, the press had very little access to information, unless someone wanted it leaked. Even then, the *Times* would have had trouble getting through to the political level that had interests in this case.

The *Times* recorded one other incident that happened in April, 1854. Part of the Grand Jury's responsibilities was to inspect the jail. This duty was to assure that there were no people in the jail who were not recorded and to assure that the jail was in acceptable condition – meaning the conditions were approaching humane.

When the jury finished its general inspection of the jail, Hegemen agreed to show them Mrs. Robinson's quarters on the upper floor. One of the members asked to see their most famous inmate. When they got to her room, they saw her sitting in her rocking chair with a veil over her head. One of the jurors began to speak to her and asked that she remove the veil. Silence. He asked again. Still silence and an eerie motionlessness. Exasperated, the juror told Hegemen to remove the veil. Being a gentleman, Hegemen refused. Finally the juror went up and lifted the veil himself. Under the veil, there was no Mrs. Robinson; instead they found her dress stuffed with the "latest Parisian fashions." Immediately there was a concern that she had fled. The assumption was that, somehow, in the confusion brought on by the inspection, she had managed to escape. She was found in a matter of seconds, given away by a "titter' of laughter coming from under her bed. When the mattress cloth was raised, she was found, laughing uncontrollably at her own little joke.

The jurors were less amused, thinking that such treatment of men with such a noble purpose as serving on the jury was "ludicrous" and "discourteous conduct." Even in the 1850's we have evidence of men assuming a level of pompous self-worth.

Trial

Day 1

On Monday, May 21, 1854, for one of the first times in America, wealth, politics, power, sex, murder and the national press all converged in one case. This trial would also provide a battle ground between newspapers that represented political parties. To the average person, all of this intrigue was minor compared to the sensation anticipated when the spicy details of an illicit relationship between adults, would be made public. The public waited eagerly to read of dealings that were usually only talked about after the children had gone to bed.

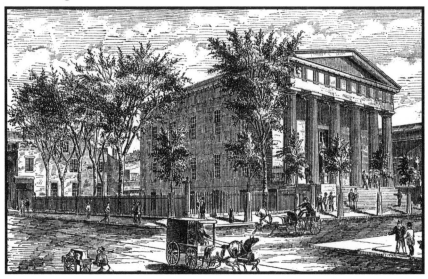

Rensselaer County Court House

Early in the afternoon, District Attorney Anson Bingham stood before Judge Ira Harris to call the case of Henrietta Robinson. By coincidence or design, it was also a few days short of the first anniversary of the poisoning of Timothy Lanagan and Catherine Lubbee. The Rensselaer County Court of Oyer and Terminer (Criminal Court) met in the old courthouse in the center of Troy. Certainly for Troy, and in many ways for all of New York State, the tribunal for Henrietta Robinson was not just a trial; it was an event. For a wide variety of reasons, such as her paramour, the mystery about who she was, the names of lawyers, and the senselessness of the murders, this trial was major news.

The telegraph was in its infancy, but it allowed news to be carried at a pace never before imagined. Reports of the events in this trial would appear in newspapers throughout the northeast as same day news.

Prior to the case of Mrs. Robinson, the court of Oyer and Terminer had been in session for over one week hearing various cases that were on the docket. The other cases, although important to those involved, had less public appeal than the case that was about to come forward. Just as today, whenever a court was going into session, a pool of jurors was called in advance and told to report to the courtroom. Except for eligibility requirements, the system has changed little in a century and a half. These potential jurors had to sit and wait to see if they were to be selected to serve on one of the juries.

Mrs. Robinson's trial was the last one for this session of the court. Preparations had been made for the trial to begin at 11:00 a.m. A problem developed when Judge Harris had the sheriff call off the names of the perspective jurors. Because of the number of jurors needed in the previous cases, by the time Mrs. Robinson's case was called, there were only eleven potential jurors remaining from the original pool. Judge Ira Harris realized the predicament and ordered the sheriff to go out and solicit an additional twenty-four potential jurors. Having given the order, the judge called a recess until 2:30 that afternoon.

It was the practice in this period for the sheriff to go into the streets and literally "pull in" potential jurors. Since to serve on a jury a person was required to be male and to own property, the pool was smaller than might be anticipated. There are stories of men pleading with a judge to be released from jury duty because they were literally driving by the courthouse, on their way to make a delivery, when the sheriff or one of his deputies took them from their wagons and pulled them into the courtroom to do their civic duty. One can imagine the effect on commerce in the neighborhood of the courthouse when court was in session. In most cases it was just like today; the last thing someone wanted to do was to be compelled to serve on a jury. Businesses near the courthouse must have seen their trade fall off radically before a trial began.

In a strategic move, District Attorney Anson Bingham and

his team had decided that, at this time, Mrs. Robinson was only to be tried for the murder of Timothy Lanagan. The case of the murder of Catherine Lubbee was held in abeyance. By having separate trials for each victim, the prosecutors gained the ability to learn the theory and strategy of the defense in the first trial. They could then prepare for those strategies if a second trial was necessary. In the event that Mrs. Robinson was found not guilty in the murder of Lanagan, Bingham still had the case of the murder of Catherine Lubbee to use later. If he were to win the case of the murder of Lanagan, then the case of Lubbee did not matter. By trying only one case at a time, the prosecution put themselves in a win-win situation.

When the court resumed at 3:00 that afternoon, the cream of the region's legal minds were all present. The defense team consisted of members from the three top law firms in Troy. All three partners of the firm of Pierson, Beach and Smith were present. There were also the members of the firm of Townsend and Olin and a very young attorney named Samuel Stover who was a partner in the firm of Stover and Jennyss, about whom we will learn much more later. During the trial, the lawyers who did the major portion of the questioning and presented the arguments for the defense were Pierson, Beach and Townsend.

The prosecution was officially led by District Attorney Anson Bingham. Knowing he could not match the defense team in the courtroom, Bingham had recruited Henry Hogeboom, of Hudson, and

George Van Santvoord

Henry Hogeboom

George VanSantvoord, a local lawyer, to handle the trial.

***

The power and presence of these men emanated throughout the courtroom as the crowd of spectators assembled. The combined charisma of these lawyers was immediately overshadowed by the entrance of the sensual woman known as Mrs. Henrietta Robinson. Those gathered watched as she walked sprightly into the room, accompanied by Sheriff John Price. Similar to the day of her arraignment, she was dressed in a stylish black silk dress, which was adorned by a hand-made collar of the finest lace; the cuffs of the dress had a similar white lace. The material for the lace alone would have cost more than most families made in a week. Although it was a little early in the season, she was wearing a white shirred bonnet, which accented her dress perfectly. In the style of the day, she had personalized the bonnet by ornamenting it with artificial flowers. It was, however, her gloves that everyone was compelled to notice. They were made of perfect white kid skin. There was not a spot on them. It was obvious that they were costly and, even more significantly, could only be worn by someone who had absolutely no intention of doing any work or carrying any of her own bags. She had chosen to appear in the costume of a refined lady. Her hands were dainty, a sign of status, since labor would have made them muscular and removed their delicacy. She was of average height, but one reporter could not resist mentioning "her fine figure," which another reporter described as being well exhibited by her selection of clothes. She also wore a black silk shawl that was accented with a white satin border.

Although all of the newspapers mentioned it that day, they did not dwell on what would become the most significant part of her wardrobe. Over her bonnet she had again placed a dark blue veil; the veil covered her face so completely that her features and expression could not be discerned. It cast a shroud over her that many felt matched the social sheath she used to cover her emotions, identity, and personal life. This was the veil that, for the length of the trial, would never be fully removed.

Before the trial actually began, the judge ordered that the deputies and other officers of the court were to keep down any noise outside the bar. The bar was the rail area in which sat all the lawyers, judges (there were three), jurors, the witness that had been called and the defendant. Judge Harris made it clear that whispering and conversation interrupted the court and would not be tolerated.

The clerk called the names of thirty-three potential jurors before a jury of twelve was impaneled. It was interesting to note that, of the twenty-one men excused from serving on the jury, nearly all fell into one of two categories. Either they admitted that they had already formed an opinion as to her guilt, or they claimed that they had not even heard of the case. It is easy to understand why either side would want to excuse someone who had already formed an opinion. However, the probable reason for excusing potential jurors who claimed not to have heard of the case is that it would

Ira Harris

have been possible only if one were a hermit. To claim that one had not heard of the case might well have meant that the person desired to be on the jury. Interestingly, not a single seated juror was from Troy; all were from the rural towns that comprised the remainder of Rensselaer County.

The problems did not end with the gathering of potential jurors. Immediately after the jury selection, District Attorney Bingham asked for a recess until the following morning because all of his witnesses were not present. Most of the prosecution's witnesses were doctors and, therefore, were working. Additionally, one of his most important witnesses, Professor Daiken, was ill. Daiken was the chemist who had examined the stomachs of the two victims. There was considerable speculation that Daiken was so ill that he would not be able to make the trial at all. Without him, the trial would have to be postponed yet again. The prosecution was mindful of *The Times* threat to delve into the reasons for any further postponements.

Judge Harris responded that he was reluctant to grant a

recess in capital cases. He noted that it was the practice of the courts, in cases of this magnitude, to sequester the jury. In effect, granting Bingham's request would have cost the county a night's lodging for each juror. In a show of conciliation, Defense Attorney Pierson said that he had no objection to allowing the jury to go home this one evening, since they had not heard any portion of the case, including the prosecution's opening.

Judge Harris listened politely to the two opposing attorneys who were in agreement on this one occasion. Harris concluded by saying that he felt it best to keep the jury together now that they had been selected; the Judge ordered that the trial could begin without the prosecution's witnesses present to hear the opening remarks.

The prosecution presented a relatively short opening statement. District Attorney Bingham passed the case to Hogeboom, who proceeded to explain, in simple terms, the case that the People, through their witnesses, were going to present. He sequenced the events of the day of the murder. He conveyed that Mrs. Robinson had been in the store three times in the morning, then, finally, for lunch. He talked about the consumption of beer at the end of lunch, adding that Mrs. Robinson had drunk some of the beer, a fact that had not been expressed prior to this. Hogeboom's first three points were expected by everyone: first, that Timothy Lanagan was murdered; second, that Mrs. Robinson possessed the poison in question; third that Mrs. Robinson had the opportunity to administer the poison. His final two points were somewhat surprising; Hogeboom, out of necessity, stretched for a motive. He cited the events the night of the dance and the denial of the two dollar loan on the morning of the murders. He also cited Mrs. Robinson's behavior upon being arrested as further evidence that she had committed the murders.

One comment made by Hogeboom in his opening remarks appears to have been the offer of a truce, since it pertained to Henrietta's lover and her family. He told the jury, "What her antecedents were, it will not be necessary at this time to inquire into." It appeared he had somehow joined in an unofficial agreement to leave a politically-connected person's name out of the court room.

When Hogeboom finished his opening remarks, it was only 6:00 p.m. He noted that his first two witnesses were not present and asked the judge for a recess until the following morning. This time the judge agreed, and the trial went into recess until 8:30 the following morning.

Knowing that this was the first day of the trial and that readers were searching for information, *The Whig* discussed Mrs. Robinson's personality, or, at the very least, her persona. According to that newspaper, Mrs. Robinson exhibited a "talent for talking," in the way she conversed with her tribe of lawyers. There was also evidence of her underlying stress. When District Attorney Bingham made his opening statement, she was uneasy and moved about in her chair.

Day 2

Many things are still uncertain about this case. However, one thing that is very clear is that Henrietta Robinson was a well-dressed defendant. On the second day, she walked brashly into court wearing a light plaid silk dress. Her gait was bold, her posture erect, and her movements controlled as she entered the courtroom. Her self-assumed authority was so great that, although she was alone, her entrance could almost have been considered a procession. As would become her trademark, her face was covered by the dark blue veil. Although they had no voice in the choice of her clothes, those who had gathered to watch the trial each day objected to the veil. They had come to see a woman charged in a double murder, not a walking shroud. The veil, however, served Mrs. Robinson's purposes well; to everyone, including the judge and jury, the veil was a mask making it impossible to see the expression of the accused.

On the second day of the trial, witnesses began to provide testimony. As straightforward as it might seem to a reader, in a trial such as this, the district attorney and his able assistants needed to begin by proving that a crime had been committed. In this case, they needed to prove that Lanagan was, in fact, murdered. Then they had to establish that the accused had access to whatever caused the death - in this instance, arsenic. The prosecution also needed to establish that the accused had the opportunity to commit the crime. Finally, they needed to show that there was a motive, a reason why the accused would murder the victim. Without a crime, access, and motive, there would be no guilt.

Dr. Adams, the physician initially called to treat Timothy Lanagan, was the first witness called by the prosecution. Dr. Adams's testimony focused on his knowledge of the victim and what happened during the last hours of Lanagan's life. Over objections from the defense, Adams added that he believed the cause of death to be a mineral poison. Dr. Adams offered a physical description of the building that the Lanagan's occupied, and noted that, during the time he was at the Lanagan's residence, Lanagan's father, mother, wife, children, sisters, and brother were all present. Dr. Adams had treated the Lanagan family for five years and knew that Lanagan was in reasonably good health. The prosecution wanted to at least suggest that Mrs. Robinson had a drinking problem which may have contributed to the murders. Therefore, it was important that Lanagan was considered by Dr. Adams to be a temperate man, that he did not drink to excess. Adams was able to testify that, to his knowledge, Lanagan did not drink to excess. He was not able to say that Lanagan did not drink at all.

Since he was the first witness, the prosecution wanted Dr. Adams to set the stage for the jury. They called on him to describe in detail the scene at the Lanagan's home, both physically and emotionally. He also talked about the events that transpired that night in the Lanagan's home. Before the jury, Dr. Adams portrayed in great detail the symptoms exhibited by Lanagan. He told the crowded courtroom how he had tried, in vain, to help the man who was experiencing an agonizing death. He testified that his conclusion that this was a case of poisoning came not only from his assessments of his patient's symptoms, but also from conversations with Mrs. Lanagan and to a limited extent, Lanagan's mother. The senior Mrs. Lanagan was not present during the incident, but was present for her son's death.

On the stand Dr. Adams testified that several times during the evening Lanagan said, "I shall not recover." Dr. Adams said he had tried to reassure Lanagan that there was some prospect for life, not because he believed there would be a recovery, but rather because he did not want his patient to give up too easily. This positive psychotherapy weakened one of the primary pieces of evidence that the prosecution wanted to have entered into the record. The district attorney's team really wanted to have Lanagan's dying declaration, more commonly referred to as a "deathbed statement", read into the record.

The theory at the time of this trial was that, in a dying declaration, a party who knew he was about to die, would have no motive to tell anything except the truth. The legal issue concerned the admissibility of a deathbed statement. Since the defense could not cross-examine a statement, a deathbed statement was only admissible if the person who provided it was certain of his or her death. Realizing that Adams's reassurances of Lanagan had hindered the ability to get Lanagan's statement into the record, the prosecution tried to show, through Adams's testimony, that a priest had been called to administer last rites. Adams could not testify that he saw a priest that evening. The most Adams would concede was that Lanagan's mother had kneeled and prayed at his bedside. Even if the room were as crowded as Adams described, it is hard to believe that he would have missed the presence of a priest.

As hard as he tried, Hogeboom could not convince the judge to allow Lanagan's statement into the record. Harris ruled that the statement was not admissible because the doctor had assured Lanagan that there was a chance he would survive. The prosecution had to settle for a statement by Adams that Lanagan had said, "A villain has destroyed me." The district attorney tried to imply that Lanagan had made the statement to Adams several times; however, under cross-examination by Beach, it was settled that the statement was only made on one occasion. Beach also wanted it to be clear that Lanagan made the statement "A villain has destroyed me," before he was sure that he was going to die, thus taking away the implication for some of the jurors that it was a modified deathbed statement. To discredit the comment, Beach questioned Dr. Adams as to the timing of the statement. The doctor told the jury that Lanagan made the statement only once approximately one half-hour after he (Adams) arrived; that would have been about 4:00 in the afternoon. There was a second point regarding the "villain" comment, that Beach wanted to make. Under Beach's careful cross-examination, Dr. Adams testified that there was never a name or even a gender ascribed to the "villain"; whoever Lanagan was referring to could have been either male or female.

It was during Dr. Adams's testimony that one of the prevailing images of this trial first surfaced. Mrs. Robinson was sitting beside the defense team, her face closely veiled and invisible to the audience, the jury or the witness. When Dr. Adams stated that he knew Mrs. Robinson before the murder, the district attorney asked him to identify her. Naturally, with her face covered by the veil, Adams could not make a positive identification. Mr. Hogeboom asked the judge to direct that the veil be removed so that the witness could make the necessary identification. The judge did as requested and asked Mrs. Robinson to remove the veil. Reluctant to be seen, Mrs. Robinson would only raise a portion of the veil for an instant. The action was so swift and carefully executed that the only people who were able to gaze upon her features were Dr. Adams and the judge. "That is the Lady," Adams swore.

Beach made only one other attempt to get this witness to provide aid to the defense. Through a series of questions, Beach tried to suggest that the death may have been the result of cholera. Dr. Adams was able to reassure everyone that, although many of the symptoms of cholera were the same as arsenic poisoning, there was no possibility that Lanagan's death was a result of cholera.

The second witness was Dr. A. J. Skilton, the second doctor called to the Lanagan's home on May 25. Dr. Skilton added little to the testimony of Dr. Adams regarding the night of the murder. There was one point to which Skilton testified to that appears to have been missed by others. Dr. Adams had testified that he stayed with Lanagan from the time he arrived until his death; Dr. Skilton said that Dr. Adams was not at the Lanagan's when he arrived at 5:00 that afternoon. If Adams was not present for a period of time, why did he leave? Even more importantly, what, if anything, happened to Lanagan during the time that Adams was out? Adams had testified that there was a period when it appeared that Lanagan was getting better. Had Adams in fact left for some reason, and, while he was gone, had someone administered the coup-de-grace?

Since, unlike Adams, Skilton was present for the autopsy, he added considerably more detail regarding its findings. If any of the farmers on the jury did not know it before, they learned from Skilton that a death by poison was painful and ugly. Dr. Skilton described in detail the effect of the poison on Lanagan's internal organs. There developed a heated debate between Skilton and

Beach over the certainty of the cause of death. Skilton claimed that, from the moment he arrived, he was certain that Lanagan had ingested a mineral poison. Skilton would not back down on his claim that he knew the cause immediately, despite Beach's ability to get him to admit that the best medical authorities of the era believed that, in the case of suspected poisoning, doctors should wait until a chemical analysis was complete before declaring it as the cause. Skilton continued to swear that he knew it was mineral poison without the benefit of chemical analysis of contents of Lanagan's stomach.

Dr. Skilton made one comment that made no sense; he testified that he had seen a white powder that looked like arsenic in Lanagan's lower stomach. He may have made that statement out of a sense of arrogance and to justify his certainty that Lanagan had died of arsenic poisoning. Assuming that Skilton told the truth about the powder, would not that have meant that the beer was not the vehicle by which the arsenic was ingested? The beer would have completely turned the arsenic from a powder to a non-discernible liquid. Future testimony would show that there was nothing visible in the beer. Second, after six hours between the ingestion of the beer and the time the stomach was removed, would not the arsenic have had to pass from the stomach, especially with the victim vomiting regularly? That is, of course, unless additional arsenic had somehow being administered while the doctors were present.

William A. Beach

Martin I. Townsend

The third witness for the prosecution was also a doctor; Dr. Seymour, along with the county coroner, Dr. Bontecou, had performed the autopsy on Lanagan. Seymour was able to show that Lanagan died as a result of severe irritation of the stomach and intestines. Since he did not do a chemical analysis of the stomach's contents, Seymour was not allowed to say positively that the irritation was the result of poison. Seymour joined Dr. Skilton in saying that there was a white powder present in the area of the lower intestines. Seymour put a measurement to the powder, saying that he did not believe it would equal a full teaspoon.

With the medical testimony over, it was time for the prosecution to place on the stand their most important witness, the aggrieved widow, Anna Lanagan. Mrs. Lanagan could have vied with Mrs. Robinson for an award for the best performance at the trial. Mrs. Lanagan, however, played the opposite role. For those gathered to watch the show, Anna Lanagan played humility to Henrietta Robinson's arrogance. Mrs. Lanagan's dress was simple and unassuming, while Mrs. Robinson's was of the best material. During the morning, as the doctors told of her husband's excruciating death, Mrs. Lanagan seemed "enfeebled and almost fainted away." This contrasted perfectly with Mrs. Robinson, who always walked with the best posture and sat straight in her chair. After Mrs. Lanagan reached the stand, it took "a considerable time" for her to collect herself before she could begin to answer the questions put to her by the prosecution. This occurred despite the fact that the prosecutors were, in their own way, her own counselors and, therefore, gentle.

An emotional Mrs. Lanagan told the jury of the events of the day of the murder. She talked about each of the five visits Mrs. Robinson made to the store. She told the jury that she had almost consumed the beer instead of her husband, implying perhaps that she was the intended victim. With considerable difficulty, Anna Lanagan told of her husband's death.

Mrs. Lanagan's testimony included a few interesting items. On at least two occasions, Mrs. Lanagan took parts of Catherine Lubbee's death statement and ascribed the incidents to herself instead of poor Catherine. For example, in Catherine Lubbee's statement, she (Catherine) said that she tried to use a spoon to take out the powdery film from the top of the glass of beer. At the trial, Mrs. Lanagan told virtually the same story, except, in Mrs. Lanagan's story, she (Anna) was the one who tried to get rid of the "scum." When the scum was being removed, Mrs. Robinson made the statement, "Don't do so, that is the best of it." As before, in Mrs. Lanagan's testimony there was a switch in the person to whom this statement was directed. Catherine in her statement to Dr. Bontecou, said that Mrs. Robinson had directed the quote to her (Catherine). On the stand, Mrs. Lanagan said that the quote by Mrs. Robinson directed the statement to her (Anna). It would seem the role of humbled martyr was not sufficient for Mrs. Lanagan; she also had to be the target of mistreatment.

Mrs. Lanagan was the only person who claimed to have seen Mrs. Robinson with the white paper. Her testimony on this point, which was accepted by the court, was critical to the prosecution.

Mrs. Lanagan was not with Catherine Lubbee when she died, so she could not testify about any of the events that transpired at her husband's cousin's house. Mrs. Lanagan's absence would play a role in the admissibility of Catherine's supposed deathbed statement.

The prosecution knew that the weakness in their case was the apparent lack of a motive. To establish some reason for such a violent act, Mrs. Lanagan was called upon to testify about the events on the night of the dance at her store. She told the jury that, because of the outburst directed at Smith, she told Mrs. Robinson to leave. Putting on the mask of the victim, Mrs. Lanagan said that, even then, she was kind enough to walk Mrs. Robinson home. In an effort to establish a motive, the prosecution steered Mrs. Lanagan to talk about Mrs. Robinson's behavior on the morning after the dance. This was the morning when Mrs. Robinson had come into the store and been so abusive to Mrs. Lanagan that it woke up Lanagan who ordered Mrs. Robinson from the store.

In their search for a motive, the prosecution also had Mrs. Lanagan testify that Mrs. Robinson had been refused a loan of two dollars on the morning of the murders. It was a stretch, but the prosecution knew that they had to reach for a reason for the poisoning. When direct examination was over, it was the general perception that Mrs. Lanagan had told her story well.

Mrs. Lanagan was a dangerous witness for the defense. A

widow, especially a humble one, could hold the hearts of the jurors. They needed to strike at her testimony without being too aggressive and, most importantly, without appearing to be uncaring. This meant that they had to change players. Beach, the master of attacking a witness and making him stumble over his own words, had cross-examined all of the witnesses thus far. When the prosecution finished with Mrs. Lanagan, Beach remained seated. Instead the defense called on the elder, calmer, more diplomatic, Job Pierson to conduct the examination of such a delicate witness.

The master of the slow waltz of words, Pierson made several key points. First, he was able to get Mrs. Lanagan to admit that, although Mrs. Robinson had stopped trading at Lanagan's for a few days, maybe even a week, after the fray at the dance, she had resumed doing business in the store subsequently. Mrs. Lanagan's own words made it appear that any wounds from the fray had mended.

It is difficult to assess the effect on the jury of Mrs. Lanagan's confusion under cross-examination. When asked by Pierson, she could not give even the month of the dance. She could not remember if they had a fiddler or a piper playing. This occurred despite the fact that she acknowledged that they only had two dances. Under Pierson's gentle hand, the defense was able to show that Mrs. Lanagan claimed to remember incredible details on some points but was not even be able to give general parameters on others. With any other witness, they would have pushed the issue of her being coached; with a grieving widow, they hoped that the jury would come to that conclusion on its own.

At one point Pierson did make it look as though any hostile feelings were the opposite of what the prosecution was trying to project. Pierson was able to get Mrs. Lanagan to admit that, on the morning of the poisoning, she did have the two dollars that Mrs. Robinson requested. Pierson, in his most tactful voice, asked Mrs. Lanagan, "Are you in the habit of lying."

"It was not much lying, what I told Mrs. Robinson," pleaded Mrs. Lanagan. Then she added one of the clearest examples of the extent of her confusion: "I did not want to refuse her or let her have the money."

There was a significant change in Mrs. Lanagan's testimony between the Coroner's inquest and the trial. At the inquest, which was held in the days immediately after her husband's death, Mrs. Lanagan told that body that there was no enmity between her family and Mrs. Robinson. In the year that had passed, she had rethought some events. At some point she decided that the incident at the dance and the failure to loan the two dollars would play better as a motive.

There was one other major point brought out in the cross-examination. It appears that Catherine Lubbee and Mrs. Robinson were very close associates, possibly even friends. The lonely Mrs. Robinson had met plain Catherine at Lanagan's. The two women had been together on several occasions in the ten days of Catherine's visit. Catherine, like the young seamstress, Mary Dillon, was in the custom of going to visit Mrs. Robinson during the day. With Mrs. Robinson's compulsion for adult company whom she could mentor and fascinate with her stories, it is more logical that she would have struggled to keep Catherine around, not to end her life.

Probably the most important testimony, to indicate that there were no ill feelings harbored after the dance, was given when Pierson was able to get Mrs. Lanagan to admit that she had visited Mrs. Robinson in her home after. Anna Lanagan had even allowed her children to visit Mrs. Robinson on several occasions.

There can be only speculation about the exact damage that Mrs. Lanagan's appearance dealt to the defense's case. She surely did not help. The poor widow struggling to raise four fatherless children can be an impressive force in a murder trial. The real problem for both sides was that she was the only witness present at the time of the alleged poisoning. The question that must be raised is: if the prosecution truly believed in the existence of a motive, why was Mrs. Lanagan the only person they put on the stand to relate any of the experiences with Mrs. Robinson and her neighbors? An objective person has to wonder why any of the other people who were in the room on the day Lanagan died, or any of the persons at the dance, were not placed on the stand to testify.

The last witness of the day was William Ostrom, the man who ran the drug store where Mrs. Robinson purchased arsenic, supposedly to kill rats. Ostrom was also the man whom she had visited on the night of her arrest. It was during Ostrom's testimony that the biggest outburst from the audience occurred. Attorney Hogeboom asked if Ostrom could identify Mrs. Robinson. Ostrom, with a touch of mockery, assured the prosecutor that he could identify her, if he could see her. Hogeboom showed his own propensity toward sarcasm as he said to Judge Harris, "I submit, your honor, we shall have to try that veil experiment one more time." There was an outburst of laughter which took several minutes for the officers of the court to control.

Harris was less amused than those gathered, but at this point he was still not willing to put the issue of the veil firmly on the table. He turned to Mrs. Robinson and said, "If the prisoner prefers it, she may step forward to where the witness is to show her face." After Mrs. Robinson moved directly in front of the witness, Ostrom assured the courtroom that the lady behind the veil was the same lady.

Ostrom's testimony focused on the purchase of the poison, the strange visit that Mrs. Robinson had made to his store on the Saturday night before her arrest. This was the evening on which he had seen her with a gun. Ostrom also spoke about her demeanor minutes before she was arrested.

Under direct examination, Ostrom testified that on May 25 Mrs. Robinson's behavior made him think that she was under the influence of alcohol. Under a skilled cross-examination by Beach, he said that the symptoms she exhibited on the night of her arrest might have been brought on by a "deranged mind." Ostrom went to say that he had no special knowledge of the effects on the body of stress or of alcohol. From the bench, Judge Harris asked a question about her normal skin color. Ostrom acknowledged that she was usually florid.

The last witness of the day was the egotistical Dr. Skilton, who was recalled. Dr. Skilton was allowed to testify as to his contacts with Catherine Lubbee on the night of the murders. He said that he saw her less than one half hour after he examined Lanagan. He saw her again immediately after Lanagan's death. He was also present for her post mortem examination. Skilton testified in no uncertain terms that he believed from the beginning that both Lanagan and Lubbee ingested mineral poison. He also said that he knew, when he saw the damage done to the stomach, that the poison used was arsenic. By the recall of Skilton, Beach had shown the depth of the young doctor's ego and did not even bother to cross-examine.

When Dr. Skilton was finished, Judge Harris recessed the trial until 8:30 the following morning. The second day of the trial, the first day of testimony, was over. Harris chose to begin the next day a full half hour earlier than most trials began; it was apparent that the judge wanted this trial over.

It was only a short walk between the courthouse and the jail. Each day Mrs. Robinson was paraded between the two buildings by a couple of officers and the Sheriff. Often, either the sheriff's wife or daughter would accompany them. In an era before paparazzi, people had to get sightings of the famous for themselves. The street between the jail and the courthouse was more crowded each day as people gathered to catch a glimpse of the woman who was coming to be known in the newspapers as "the veiled murderess."

Mrs. Robinson's reaction to the growing crowds was somewhat surprising. Rather than seeking additional protection or the shelter of a carriage, she asked that she be allowed to walk by herself with the officers following at a safe distance. Naturally, Price rejected this, and she continued to make the trip among a gaggle of officers.

Day 3

Court began at the early hour of 8:30 a.m. After the officers of the court finished calling the role, it became obvious that Judge Harris had been deliberating over his options regarding Mrs. Robinson's veil. Although he had heard sarcastic comments from lawyers and witnesses, and even though remarks about the veil had caused outbursts of laughter, Judge Harris had maintained his patience when it came to Mrs. Robinson's facial curtain. He began the morning by remarking that for two days the prisoner had been allowed to remain "masked." He continued, "We have had the singular spectacle of a prisoner on trial, charged with a high capital crime without the Jury or the Court ever having seen that prisoner." Harris went on to remind those gathered that it may only seem like a "matter of ceremony", but it was the form prescribed by law for the jury to "look upon the prisoner and the prisoner upon the jury." Harris went on to say that he felt a "repugnance" at "trying a prisoner whose face had never been seen." At that point Harris commanded that Mrs. Robinson remove the veil.

"I am here to undergo a most painful and important trial. I do not wish to be gazed at." Responded Mrs. Robinson when Judge Harris decreed that she reveal her face.

In considering Mrs. Robinson's comment, Harris admitted that his request might be a hardship, "but it is not one for which the court is responsible." He left his order in place.

Mrs. Robinson did not move. The veil remained steadfastly in place. There, in front of a hushed court room, a battle of wills had begun. For long, tense moments, silence prevailed.

A true gentleman of the Victorian strain, Harris eventually broke the stalemate, "We shall use no coercion Mrs. Robinson, but, unless you remove your veil so that your face may be seen by the jury, we shall regard you of refusing compliance with a just and reasonable demand of the court."

Understanding the impact that a refusal, of what must be considered a reasonable request, could have on the jury, William Beach rose to address the judge: "Your Honor, we have advised with the prisoner and earnestly urged and entreated her to comply with the suggestions of the court, her reply to us is, that rather than sit here unveiled, she had rather incur any hazard, however great, and endure all possible consequences. The court will perceive that we are powerless in the matter."

There was an uncomfortable pause as the judge stared at the dark blue shroud covering Mrs. Robinson's face. It was a question of who would blink, judge or defendant. Judge Harris finally turned to the lawyers and said, "Proceed with the case."

The first witness of the morning was Officer Charles Burns of the Troy Police Department. Burns was the officer who had arrested Mrs. Robinson one year earlier in the cabinet shop. He told the court, that, after Mrs. Robinson was assured that he was an officer, she walked with him to the jail. One of the points that the prosecution wanted from this witness was her mood during the walk to the jail. Burns related that she had laughed and joked along the way. The prosecution wanted her attitude on the record because, if she were the murderer, this conduct could seem symptomatic of someone who is totally callous to a heinous act.

Burns responded to the prosecution's second line of questioning by stating that, at the jail, Sheriff Price, another deputy, and he had taken two pistols from Mrs. Robinson. Burns stressed the term "took" the pistols, making it clear that Mrs. Robinson did not want to part with them, even when she was in the safety of police custody. No one questioned why Burns had not taken the pistols when he and Mrs. Robinson were still in the cabinet shop. At this time, it was extremely rare for a woman of culture to ever touch a pistol, let alone to carry one on her person. Knowing that she was armed left the jury with two possible conclusions – that she was either a dangerous person or a person fearful for her own safety.

The third line of questioning dealt with the search of Mrs. Robinson's house; Burns testified that he was one of the men who searched the little house "from garret to basement" on the night of the murders. He told the jury that he found the packet of arsenic under the rug. When asked, Burns noted that the rug was nailed in place, thus making access to the poison a challenge, not an accident.

The prosecution saved their trump card, from Burns's deck of knowledge, for last. Burns said that at the jail, he had found a piece of white paper in Mrs. Robinson's pocket. (The druggist had already testified that he wrapped the arsenic in white paper). Mrs. Lanagan said that she had seen Mrs. Robinson with a piece of white paper. When asked what happened to the paper, Burns said that there was nothing on it, so he threw it away (Ostrom, the druggist had said that he marked both pieces of paper).

Beach's cross examination indicated that the defense was moving ever closer to an insanity defense. Beach managed to have Burns admit that, during the walk to the jail, Mrs. Robinson had talked "lightly", implying that she did not see any reason to be anxious about the events that were unfolding. During that walk, she was concerned about two things: her appearance and whether she were being taken to the recorder's office. Burns said that he had reassured her about her looks, saying that he thought that she looked presentable, especially given that it was a rainy day. Burns opened the door to consideration of Mrs. Robinson's mental confusion when he said that they were walking in exactly the opposite direction from the recorder's office, and Mrs. Robinson did not seem to care.

Beach then went into the topic of the search of her home, asking if anything else was found under the carpet besides a packet of arsenic; Burns gave an affirmative answer. Under pressure from Beach, Burns expanded his answer, adding that there was also a packet of paper with Spanish fly (believed at the time to be a sexual stimulant), a box of jewelry, a watch and a locket. Mrs. Robinson motioned for Beach to come to her side; Beach bent closer, she whispered something in his ear. Beach stood up and continued with the witness, "My client wishes to know what became of her locket?" Lockets, then as now, opened and usually had a picture of someone inside.

Burns responded in a second, "Dr. Bontecou took charge of everything, including the keys to her house."

There were three more points Beach wanted to make to demonstrate that Mrs. Robinson was not thinking clearly when it came to her personal safety. He tried to accomplish this by getting Burns to admit that she was reluctant to give up the pistols, even though she was in police custody; if she felt safe, why would she need the guns. Secondly, Beach put emphasis on the fact that she was allowed to walk up the block alone. If she were thinking clearly (as the prosecution implied with respect to the guns), why had she not disposed of the paper? Beach's implication was that the paper Burns found was innocent. Finally, Burns testified that she seemed surprised at being inside the jail; if she did not understand that she was under arrest, why had she walked with the officer, and if she did understand, why was she surprised to be at the jail?

When Burns was given back to the prosecution for redirect, two different attorneys attacked the points that they believed Beach had made successfully. Van Santvoord wanted to clarify that Mrs. Robinson was not acting strangely when she was arrested. Burns said that she was not acting strangely, for a woman under arrest. Remember, at this time, most women were arrested either for public intoxication or for prostitution; one can only guess what "acting normally" under arrest meant to Burns. Beach elicited testimony that, at the time Burns found Mrs. Robinson, she was leisurely shopping, not something one would expect from a person accused of poisoning two people. Under questioning by Hogeboom,

Burns acknowledged that she was shopping, but could not say what she was looking at.

It would be hard to judge the effect of Burns's testimony. He had witnessed and described Mrs. Robinson's behavior on the evening in question; he had searched her house, but he was a police officer, not a doctor. If it came to a question of insanity, the jury would have to determine if his perceptions of rational behavior were more accurate than those of the doctors.

The next witness, Burr Lord, added nothing, factually, to the case. His contribution was more an appeal to the emotions of the jury. Lord was a partner in the grocery store where Lanagan had gone after lunch on the day he was poisoned. He talked about Lanagan's appearance that fateful day, stressing the external symptoms of the poison.

It was only logical that Dr. Reed Bontecou, the coroner, be called as a witness by the prosecution. On direct examination, he testified to the search of Mrs. Robinson's person, her house and to what had transpired while he was at Lanagan's store, including the convening of the inquest. Most important to the prosecution was his testimony relating to taking the statement about Timothy Lanagan from Catherine Lubbee. The prosecution wanted her statement before the jury. One of the best pieces of evidence they could have hoped for was a deathbed statement. What they regarded as Lanagan's deathbed statement had not been admitted; now they definitely wanted Catherine's statement entered into evidence. The problem was that when Dr. Bontecou took her statement, he sincerely believed that she might recover. He had not taken her statement as a deathbed statement, but as evidence to be used at the inquest into the death of Timothy Lanagan. "Deathbed" meant that the person knew she was dying; Catherine Lubbee had not been told that she would not recover. Try as they might, Judge Harris refused to allow the statement into evidence.

Under direct examination, Bontecou also testified about the autopsy, about the condition of Lanagan's stomach, and about finding the granules of arsenic in the upper intestine.

Whether he intended to or not, Bontecou added a degree of levity to the trial. Apparently after a portion of the sugar was tested and found not to contain arsenic, Bontecou used the rest himself. It was his testing of the beer that made people chuckle. It seems that Bontecou and some members of the coroner's jury felt that it was imperative for the beer to be tested. Their method was foolproof. They drank samples of the beer (there is no description of the sample sizes) to be sure that it was not tainted. Note: they did not test the sugar in the same way.

It was, however, during the cross-examination, under the skillful inquisition by Beach, that Bontecou made his biggest impact. So powerful was Beach's method that, by the time Bontecou's testimony was done, he almost became a defense witness. Bontecou told the jury of his impressions of Mrs. Robinson on the night she was arrested, and on his visits with her in her cell over the course of the following few weeks. He said that on the first night she was not intoxicated, but seemed effected by extreme anxiety. He was the only doctor who saw her that night, and the defense felt that his testimony should play heavily on the jury. He said that she did not answer direct questions but rather would ramble on and on in meaningless conversation. He even testified that, on one occasion, he told her that she was accused of killing Lanagan and Lubbee. According to Bontecou, she showed no signs of even acknowledging his comment. In Bontecou's mind, Mrs. Robinson was not rational, and he made that clear to the jury.

Through Beach's questioning, it was revealed that Bontecou had been to her cell several times during the three weeks following the murders. His visits had been short in duration, usually about fifteen minutes, but they were frequent, two to three times per week.

When it was time for redirect examination, the prosecution was left with a serious dilemma. Bontecou had testified that Mrs. Robinson was not drunk on the night of her arrest, but she was irrational, thus setting the stage for an insanity defense. Because of Beach's questioning of Bontecou, the prosecution was now in a position of having to impeach its own witness. To offset his observations, they needed to create the appearance that Bontecou was somehow tainted. The prosecution needed to show that Bontecou had somehow become infatuated with Mrs. Robinson, and therefore he could not reasonably judge her state of mind. Hogeboom decided that the best impeachment of Bontecou's observations would be based on the number of visits he made to Mrs. Robinson's cell.

Under cross examination, Bontecou said that he had visited her to talk about the disposition of her property. Obviously, the prosecution wanted to show that Mrs. Robinson had somehow placed the young doctor under some form of mystical charm. Her ability to have men under her spell was a different twist from anything that had been put forward before, but it would reappear again, soon and often. From this point forward, Hogeboom held that she had some power over men; he felt it was some sort of curse she could apply at will.

"Will you inform us what inducements led you to visit a crazy woman two or three times a week about her property?", asked Hogeboom, the sarcasm evident in his tone and question.

"There were no inducements held out to me sir! I had the keys to her house". Dr. Bontecou had his reputation on the line; he was not going to let this out-of-town lawyer attack his credibility. Bontecou claimed that his visits were necessary because he was responsible for her possessions and, for that reason only, he visited her. He reiterated that, as soon as custody of her property was taken over by someone else, he did not return to her cell.

Hogeboom then attacked Bontecou's lack of experience in diagnosing insanity. Bontecou acknowledged that mental illness was not part of his regular practice, but went on to say that on more that twenty occasions he had been called upon to assist in the diagnosis of insanity. Most of these cases did not involve any criminal actions, but involved people from the alms-house or private hospitals.

Bontecou could only recall one instance in which Mrs. Robinson even acknowledged the existence of the Lanagans, when he told her that Mrs. Lanagan wanted her pot and other personal items returned. These items, belonging to Mrs. Lanagan, were in Mrs. Robinson's home; their being found in her possession raises a question that was never asked. Obviously, the only way a boiling pot could have gotten there was either by loan, or by being brought over full. If full, it meant that Mrs. Lanagan was cooking for Mrs. Robinson; if borrowed, it meant that the families were on such close terms that Mrs. Lanagan was comfortable lending to Mrs. Robinson. The bonnet could have only been left at Mrs. Robinson's if it had been worn into her house by Mrs. Lanagan or Catherine Lubbee. The location of these items clearly indicated the closeness of the two families. What is not clear is the reason why the defense did not explore an explanation for cooking utensils belonging to the Lanagan's being in Mrs. Robinson's house.

As he stepped down from the witness stand, it was hard to tell how Bontecou's testimony had impacted the jury. His words were close to impartial. The impression he had on the jury would have been created by his delivery.

Bontecou impacted the trial dramatically in another unforeseen way. Through Bontecou's testimony, Beach had approached the issue of insanity. Unexpectedly, Harris directed Beach to stop this line of questioning. Harris told Beach in no uncertain terms that, if the defense was going to be based on insanity, then the jury had an "obligation" to look upon the face of the accused. It was their responsibility to see her expressions so that they might judge her sanity for themselves.

Harris had finally established his line in the sand. Either Mrs. Robinson would have to remove the veil, or they could not question any further on the issue of insanity. Beach argued that he had implored Mrs. Robinson to remove the veil, but she refused. Harris held firm. For a second time that day, the courtroom was at a standoff. Finally, Mrs. Robinson lifted the front of the veil; for a few moments her face was exposed to the jury and judge. In his own mind Harris had finally won the issue of Mrs. Robinson and the veil. It may have been a reluctant move, but she had removed the covering from the front of her face. She replaced the veil almost immediately by shielding her face with her fan. The change was so fast that only those whose gaze was fixed on her caught even the slightest glimpse of her face. At last the veiled murderess was not veiled, but neither was her face visible to anyone in the court. Later that day, she would use a handkerchief to cover her lower face. As the day went on, she slowly pulled the veil back over her face.

Dr. Skilton was recalled to allow him to explain again his certainty that it was arsenic poisoning, when there had been no chemical analysis completed while he was present. It was obvious that his reappearance was intended to reinforce the doctor's ego. Beach did not even bother to cross examine, as though he knew that the doctor's additional words had no impact on the jury.

The final witness for the prosecution was Professor Daikin,

a chemist who lived in Albany. Daikin was the regional expert on poison. As such, he was involved in most investigations in which the victim was suspected of having died as the result of the use of poison. Daikin and Bontecou, working together, had examined Lanagan's stomach. Daikin testified to the presence of lesions caused by a poison. He also explained the test he had performed on the white grains that were found in Lanagan's stomach. His test proved conclusively that, somehow, Lanagan had ingested a large amount of arsenic. He had also tested the sugar found in Lanagan's store. Daikin testified that there was no arsenic found in the sugar.

***

To prove their case, the prosecution had called a total of nine witnesses; four were doctors (Adams, Skilton, Seymour, and Bontecou). Three of the doctors were involved either in the treatment of Lanagan and Lubbee or in the autopsy. The fourth doctor, Reed Bontecou, because of his association with the police, was also involved in the search of Mrs. Robinson's home. The remaining witnesses were:

- The druggist who sold Mrs. Robinson some arsenic
- The grocer who saw Lanagan in pain
- The professor of Chemistry who determined the cause of death to be arsenic
- The Police officer who arrested Mrs. Robinson Mrs. Lanagan.

Unable to have the "deathbed" statement of Catherine Lubbee admitted into evidence, the prosecution had indirectly lost one additional witness.

The selection of people whom the prosecution failed to call as witnesses is perplexing. Is it significant that Old-Man-Haley, who lived in the same house as Mrs. Robinson, and William Buckley, who had helped to carry Lanagan to the bed, never testified? Why had the prosecution called a merchant, Burr Lord, to talk about Lanagan's early symptoms, yet not called any members of his family who were with him when he died? Even better, why had they not called Buckley, who was not family? The prosecution had a year to plan this case; why were so few people called? The only logical explanation is that these witnesses, like Bontecou, would have ultimately become more beneficial for the defense.

When the prosecution rested on the third day, they had proven most of their case. Through the testimony of the doctors and chemist, they had proven beyond a reasonable doubt that Lanagan was poisoned; the case for Lubbee was not in question during this trial, although they had also proven that she was poisoned. Through the druggist's testimony the prosecution had established that Mrs. Robinson had access to arsenic. Through Mrs. Lanagan's testimony they had shown that Mrs. Robinson had access to the sugar and, therefore, to the beer, so she could have mixed the arsenic into the drink. There was one huge gap in the case. As hard as they tried, the prosecution was not able to establish a motive, and to kill two people without a motive would be an insane act. These were the thoughts of the defense as they caucused during the break.

During the extended lunch break, the team of defense lawyers discussed at length whether to even put forward a defense. Their problem was in trying to guess whether the prosecution's hole, lack of motive, was big enough for their client to slip through. There was one other very touchy issue that they contemplated. Unless either Catherine Lubbee or Timothy Lanagan had committed suicide, Mrs. Lanagan was the only other logical suspect, and to attack the grieving widow might appear to the jury to be malicious. There was also the problem of addressing Mrs. Lanagan's motive for such a horrendous act. Since Lanagan was hardly rich, the only motive for Mrs. Lanagan would have been jealousy, but there was no proof of a physical or emotional relationship between Catherine and Lanagan. There was also no concrete proof that such a relationship did not exist.

***

At 3:00 p.m., Job Pierson made the defense's opening statement to the jury. Pierson proudly acknowledged that he was the oldest of the attorneys in the room. He used his age as a crutch, speaking in a sage-like way, much like a well-educated grandfather. He reminded the jury that he had been, at one time, the District Attorney, like Bingham, he had to prosecute cases of murder. Pierson, however, quickly separated himself from Bingham and his out-of-town hired man, Hogeboom. Pierson told the jury that he had not tried to use evidence inappropriately. He had never tried to get into evidence a statement that was not a true deathbed statement, a reminder that Hogeboom had done exactly that. He went on to say that the defense counsel had nothing to expect from this poor woman, Mrs. Robinson, since they were not being paid. The fact that she was represented by the best lawyers in Troy, and that they claimed to be providing their services for free, added to the mystery of the identity of Mrs. Robinson.

Pierson said that he had never met Mrs. Robinson before being introduced to her in jail. He learned of her arrest from a jailer. The jailer, when he first came for Pierson, said that he thought she was acting insane. Pierson told the jury that he felt it was his duty to go and see her. His impressions were the same as the jailer's; she did appear to be a "perfect maniac." In his best descriptive tone, he continued, "Her mind was tottering and reason was dethroned." Only weeks after his first visit was Pierson able to get her to help with her defense. Pierson went on with his assertions on her sanity, "Indeed gentlemen, the conduct (here) in Court shows you that she is not right in her mind. I do not say, or believe, she is insane, but her mind has lost its balance in a degree." It was Pierson's contention that, from before the murders until several weeks later, she was insane, but now she was back on a more even course.

At this point, Pierson got in his best shot against the prosecution. He claimed that, through their statements and questions, they had appeared as witnesses themselves. Pierson went on to point out that, if there had been representation at the grand jury, Mrs. Robinson would probably never have been charged with the crime of which she stood accused.

Pierson then went into the issue of the long discussion by the attorneys over whether or not to close the case without calling a single witness. Several on the team thought that the prosecution had simply failed to prove, beyond a reasonable doubt, that Mrs. Robinson placed the poison in the drinks. Those same lawyers felt that, based on the prosecution's case, there would be either an acquittal or a verdict of "not guilty by reason of insanity". There were others on the team who believed that there was even more, and stronger, evidence of insanity that should be put before the jury. Pierson then went on for some time expounding on that evidence and which witness would be giving the relevant testimony.

Almost as an afterthought, Pierson went back to the lack of evidence that Mrs. Robinson had placed the poison in the beer. He returned to a theme that he and the rest of the team would stress over and over – the complete lack of any motive. Pierson reminded the jury that every person ever tried for murder in Rensselaer County had a motive presented. In Pierson's words, "I may be permitted to say that there is no human being to give color to the suspicion that Mrs. Robinson put poison in the beer; except Mrs. Lanagan." He paused letting the impact of the statement settle upon the jury. "And what does she say? Why, she says that she saw a white paper in the hands of Mrs. Robinson. This is all." Pierson was demonstrating the painful lack of evidence that the prosecution had put forward. "But what is the theory that the prosecution counsel will ask you to adopt? It is that the white paper contained the poison; and that Mrs. Robinson mixed the poison in the sugar and then in the beer." When considered in terms of the number of steps, the murder became rather complex.

It was at this point that Pierson played the only reasonable card. This was the one that no one wanted to see, but, at the same time, the only explanation that seemed logical. "I wish not to attack the character of any human being; but we must look at things as they are." He was about to address the issue of motive, and everyone knew it. "Who was Miss Lubbee? An unmarried woman; and who is Mrs. Robinson?" Pierson answered his own question. "A woman residing in the neighborhood, spending much of her time at the house of Lanagan," for a moment he faced the accused, then he continued, "and a pretty woman to say the least. Jealousy, gentlemen, sometimes goes a great ways. Certain it is that Mrs. Lanagan did not drink the beer." Another pause, "I am justified in saying that she did not at any time intend to drink it." This last comment was a gross understatement; she, in her own statements, had stressed that she did not like beer. "I cast no aspersions. My duty and purpose is to defend this truly unfortunate woman." He had succeeded in presenting the only logical explanation for the crime; the reasonable defendant would have been Mrs. Lanagan, not Mrs. Robinson. He went on to compliment the jury in the style of the day. "This case I am not afraid to entrust to the hands of this or any other intelligent jury."

***

The first witness for the defense was, to say the least, an interesting character. His name was William Hegemen, a man who was both a physician and one of the sheriff's deputies. To add to his unique position as a witness, Hegemen also resided in the jail.

Dr. Hegemen summarized his impressions that Mrs. Robinson was irrational. To substantiate his conclusion, he cited examples of her behavior while in the jail. Some of the examples he gave were: the breaking up and burning of her fine furniture, her constant obsession about her appearance, and the terrible fears she had during the first few nights in the jail.

To counter the argument that Mrs. Robinson was an alcoholic, Hegemen assured the jury that Mrs. Robinson had not consumed any alcohol during the entire summer following her arrest. It was in the use of alcohol as a medicine that Hegemen made some interesting findings. He noted that he has often prescribed wine and brandy in the fall and winter for medicinal purposes, but never ardent spirits. He also told the court that, although she had often asked for various drinks, Mrs. Robinson had never once asked for beer, implying that beer was not her drink of choice, and, therefore a likely reason that she had not consumed beer when Catherine Lubbee and Lanagan ate their fateful lunch.

Hegemen also testified that he knew almost nothing of the night she took the poison, as he was away from the jail.

Under cross-examination, Hogeboom went back to his theme that Mrs. Robinson had men under some kind of spell. Hogeboom started by making Hegemen state again that he was only twenty-six. In Hogeboom's mind, the younger the man, the stronger was Mrs. Robinson's spell.

In an effort to embarrass Hegemen, Hogeboom went back to the issue of Mrs. Robinson's dress. He made Hegemen admit that he had seen Mrs. Robinson in her night clothes; at that time, immodesty on the part of a woman was a morally condemnable offense. Most important for the prosecution, they were able to get him to admit that he was not an expert on insanity. He was not totally unfamiliar with legal issues involving insanity; during his career he had been involved in three previous cases dealing with prisoners considered to be mentally unsound. The prosecution attacked his lack of formal study of insanity.

When asked if the breaking up of her furniture was the act of an insane person, Hegemen said that it was not, if considered as a single act, but when taken in the context of the fact she was not angry at anyone, nor was she in need of heat, he thought it did indicate an imbalance.

***

The second witness was Mary Dillon, the young seamstress from down the street. Like Hegemen, Mary was called to testify as to Mrs. Robinson's mental state. The difference is that Hegemen testified about her state of mind after May 25 while Mary testified as to the state before May 25. On direct examination, Mary testified regarding the dress alteration incident and the two different stories about who had originally cut the material. Then she discussed their friendship and that Mrs. Robinson had spoken of being able to swim and that she would be a "grand soldier." She told the jury that Mrs. Robinson's stories regarding her past changed even more often than her clothes. Most importantly, she told the jury that, after a while, she became afraid of Mrs. Robinson.

Mary told of Mrs. Robinson's coming over one night to have Mary's older sister get Dr. Boswell; Mrs. Robinson claimed that she needed him to treat her sick husband who had just come home. Mary testified that, minutes later, Mrs. Robinson said the real reason she wanted Dr. Boswell was so that she (Mrs. Robinson) could "blow his brains out."

Mary told at length about Mrs. Robinson's fixation on the alleged slander by the Boutwells, and about, the time that she had shown up in the morning dressed only in her night clothes.

Mary was not finished testifying when Judge Harris noted that the hour was late and ordered a recess until the next day.

***

In terms of strategic decisions, this had been a very important day for all the parties. Harris had ultimately won the contest of the veil. He won, not because he was obnoxious or demanding, but because he had been cunning and knew when to use his trump card. The prosecution rested after calling a minimal number of witnesses. Their whole case rested on the testimony of one person, Mrs. Lanagan. The defense, in a mixed decision, had chosen to put on an insanity defense. The election of an insanity defense would have to suggest to some of the jurors that there had to be guilt; if not, why use an insanity defense.

There is one very important legal point of which the reader must be mindful. Today we assume that anyone can testify in his or her own defense. That was not the case in the 1850's. The laws in this country are based on British Common Laws, and not until an amendment to the State Constitution in 1867 could a person testify in his own defense. It would be another forty years before a person could testify in England. In this case, Mrs. Robinson could not testify to her side of the story, so having Mrs. Lanagan as the only witness may have seemed adequate, although they would have been better off with Catherine Lubbee's last statement. Before judging the lack of a person's testimony too harshly, there was a feeling later that more people were convicted based on their own testimony than were ever found not guilty based on their own words.

Day Four

All of the newspaper reports anticipated that the trial would end by noon on the fourth day. There did not seem, to the reporters covering the trial, that there was much more evidence to enter into the record. The reporters were wrong.

Anthony Goodspeed, the butcher in the market where Mrs. Robinson had tried to purchase the game, was the first witness of the day. He was put on the stand to testify to the extremes of her behavior. He had seen her repeat herself, and he had seen her well-turned calf; both were behaviors that would be considered to be out of the norm. It was also to Goodspeed that Mrs. Robinson had claimed to have sworn out the summons against her neighbors.

The prosecution tried to establish that the summons to which Mrs. Robinson referred was against the men who worked at the dam, not against her neighbors. This was probably in an effort to show that her issue was with men, not everyone. When asked for a clarification, Goodspeed said that she never gave the names, so he could not confirm or deny the identity of the persons for whom the summons were issued.

Young Mary Dillon was recalled to undergo cross examination by George VanSantvoord. The prosecution was trying to dispel the defense's position that Mrs. Robinson was insane. They went after Mary by questioning why, if Mrs. Robinson's behavior was so outrageous, had she continued the relationship, and, more importantly why had this young lady allowed the relationship to become so intimate.

They were, in effect, trying to illustrate a progression. Mrs. Robinson's behavior around Mary began as "different" and evolved to outlandish. Mary told the jury about her relationship with Mrs. Robinson, how it started with Mrs. Robinson asking to have her clothes repaired and, ultimately, with Mrs. Robinson showing up at Mary's house in her night clothes. The jury also saw a young girl of humble means being allowed to become intimate with a worldly woman. This was a woman who opened the young woman's eyes to the glamour of the world of the elite.

The last portion of Mary's testimony raised the biggest fuss. She was asked to name anyone whom she had seen at Mrs. Robinson's. She named a couple of neighbors, including Mrs. Lanagan's sister (not Catherine Lubbee, who was a sister-in-law). The final person Mary described raised the emotional level of the court. Mary could not name the man for sure; he was in the other room, but she had seen him clearly. At first Mrs. Robinson said that the man was her husband. Later, she said it was a Dr. Potter from Albany. Regardless of his name, he was middle-aged and well dressed.

The redirect only focused on Mary reminding the jury that she did not believe that she had often seen Mrs. Robinson the worse for drinking liquor.

Before the next witness was called, the defense team caucused at the table. During the ensuing conversation with her lawyers, for the only time during the trial, Mrs. Robinson did not try to cover her face. No recess was called, yet she and her attorneys consulted at their table for nearly thirty minutes. Her gestures were violent and, at one point, she shed tears. Even though her voice could not be heard, it was evident that she was extremely upset. For the first time, and in a different way, Mrs. Robinson had just given evidence to the jury.

Edwin Brownell, the next witness, added one of the most significant twists with his testimony. Brownell was the Overseer of the Poor who had met with Mrs. Robinson in early May, before the murders. He was the man who had visited the chief of police on her behalf. Brownell reported, in detail, the visit that she made to his office. He told of her fears about her neighbors. He also told of having seen her a week later near a boarding house on the corner near Ferry and Second Streets. The real shock occurred when, on the stand and at the urging of the defense, Brownell uttered the name of John C. Mather. Until the moment he said the name in court, the positive link between Mather and Robinson had not been made. Everyone in Troy presumed the connection, but references to it were according to a strict Victorian code, in which everyone knew, and everyone winked, but no one ever stated the connection out loud.

Under cross-examination, Brownell testified about being at her house on the night she visited his office. In an effort to show premeditation, the prosecution brought out the fact that she had, in her home, the guns and the powder and wadding to load them. Brownell said that she pointed to a pile of shirts that were stacked on one of the chairs; she told him that the shirts belonged to Mather. Brownell told the jury that he took her at her word and did not look for laundry marks.

The prosecutors made one mistake. In an effort to show that Mrs. Robinson was unnecessarily afraid, they asked Brownell for the names of the two men whom she had mentioned in his office. Brownell could only remember one name, but he was sure that name was Gillespie, who had since gone to prison. The implication was that Gillespie was a man of whom she had a right to be wary.

Moses Warren was put on the stand to try to establish a more specific date when Mrs. Robinson had visited Edwin Brownell's office. Warren was acquainted with John C. Mather. Like Mather, Warren had been in Washington in May. He remembered that he and Mather had taken the same train from Washington on May 20 or 21. Brownell claimed that it was two weeks before Mather's return when Mrs. Robinson first came to his office; that would have put her in his office on approximately May 10, which was at about the same time that she purchased the poison.

John Knickerbacker was called upon to show that Mrs. Robinson's behavior was odd in the days before the murders.

Knickerbacker told the jury about the night that he met Mrs. Robinson on the street, and she had confronted him with a gun. The Knickerbacker family had a very high profile history in Rensselaer County. John had the right surname to impact any jury, but his message was limited.

When Knickerbacker finished, it was close to the noon hour. The defense announced that they were considering resting their case. They wanted time to confer among themselves and requested that the judge grant a recess. Harris called a recess until 2:30; the date was May 25, and, during this recess, the first anniversary of the poisoning passed. The year had been a roller coaster ride for most of those involved in this case, but for none more than for Henrietta Robinson.

When the lunch break was over, the defense had changed its mind and wanted to place two more witnesses on the stand.

The defense started the afternoon by recalling Dr. Hegemen, the combination doctor and deputy. It was now obvious that the defense was planning to lean heavily on the issue of insanity, so Hegemen was asked about Mrs. Robinson's behavior on the first night that she was in jail. He also told the jury that, the first morning, he had to use force to restrain Mrs. Robinson in order to get out of her cell. That was the morning on which she imagined that there were people in the surrounding cells.

According to Hegemen, as he tried to leave her cell, Mrs. Robinson grabbed him, refusing to let go. He told the jury that the only way he could get out of the cell was to "disengage myself by force."

There was one last portion of Hegemen's testimony on redirect. He related that Mrs. Robinson was visited by R. C. Jennyss and his law partner, Storer.

On cross-examination, the prosecution attacked Hegemen, implying that he worked as a spy for the defense and for others with a special interest in the trial. Hogeboom began by implying that his recall to the witness chair was a result of input he had given to the defense during the break. Hegemen said that he had met only with Olin, one of the assisting lawyers and a partner of Townsend. Hegemen was also asked how often he reported to Jennyss or his partner about Mrs. Robinson's behavior, to which he responded "occasionally when I met them." The prosecution also went into the use of snuff, asking how much and how often Hegemen had bought it for Mrs. Robinson. Hegeman said that, during the year, he had purchased two to three pounds of snuff for Mrs. Robinson.

The second witness that afternoon was Richard Jennyss, an attorney and partner of Storer, a member of Mrs. Robinson's defense team. If R.C. Jennyss was anything, he was articulate. His story on the witness stand was one of the most colorful in a trial laced with vivid tales. Jennyss related that, when he visited Mrs. Robinson in her cell, she told him of both the mob and of the couple who were going to boiler her in the jail.

In an entirely new twist, Jennyss reported that he had seen Mrs. Robinson, about three or four weeks before the murders, in the office of Mr. Robertson, the City Recorder. He said that, at the time, she looked very agitated, and she was "wild in appearance and her conversation incoherent." After she left, he remarked to Mr. Robertson about her "state of mind."

This case was filled with stress and, once the testimony began, emotions ran high. As in all stressful situations, people were looking for something to alleviate the anxiety. Humor is often one of the best remedies. It is doubtful that, as Jennyss went to the witness chair, he thought he would be the source of levity.

There is nothing a trial lawyer, who is bitter over an issue, enjoys more than the fantasy of placing one of his adversaries on the stand. To Hogeboom, Jennyss was meat about to be devoured. As the defense had turned the prosecution witness, Dr. Bontecou, into a defense witness, Hogeboom wanted nothing more than to turn Jennyss into his witness.

Hogeboom began his attack by establishing Jennyss's relationship to the accused. Jennyss was, after all, the partner of Storer, the counsel who had sat beside Beach, Townsend and Pierson throughout the trial. Under cross-examination, Jennyss said that he had visited Mrs. Robinson, not as her counsel or even in the capacity of a lawyer; he had gone to see her as a friend of someone else. Hogeboom made Jennyss admit that he had gone to her cell on behalf of John C. Mather. Jennyss pointed out that, when he visited Mrs. Robinson, he was not in Mather's employment nor were the visits at Mather's request. Jennyss said that he had gone to see

Mrs. Robinson merely out of friendship to Mather. By not being a counsel, his testimony was not protected by lawyer-client privilege.

When pressed on two points, these visits took on a different tone. As to the term of the visits, Jennyss said at first that they lasted ten days to two weeks. He then said that they went on for a month. When asked for the duration of the motive for his visit, Jennyss responded, "The motive that actuated me in going there, on my first visit, ceased at the expiration of a week or ten days." Pressed about why he continued to go, Jennyss said, "It was from motives of curiosity."

With the word "curiosity", Hogeboom had his opening, "How long did your curiosity last?" The courtroom rang out with laughter. Again Hogeboom would raise the specter of Mrs. Robinson having a power over young men; Jennyss was only thirty-two at the time of the trial.

The two attorneys came to a draw on the issue of Mrs. Robinson's response to Jennyss's visits. Hogeboom asked what her feelings were. Jennyss responded, "I could get no intelligent response from her." Jennyss did not seem too imposing, but he did become one more witness to say that she was irrational shortly after her arrest.

Having Jennyss admit that he had come as a friend of Mather opened up other doors. In response to one of Hogeboom's questions, Jennyss said that he had never seen Mather and Mrs. Robinson together. If he had not seen them together, and if Mather had not requested that he visit her, why did he think there was a relationship? Jennyss responded, "I had heard his name made use of in connection with hers prior to the arrest." The motive for the visits now was a major question. Jennyss admitted that he had heard that Mrs. Robinson had letters from Mather. Jennyss explained, "To avoid the scandal that might arise from the exposure of those letters, I went to her to see if I could get them."

Over the course of a series of questions, the status of the letters was determined. Jennyss's main reason for going to see Mrs. Robinson had been to get back the letters. During his visit on the first day, he told her what he wanted, but she consistently seemed unresponsive. After a couple of weeks, she said that he could have the letters. He asked her to sign an order directing

Dr. Bontecou to give him the letters; this was during the time that Bontecou was responsible for her belongings. Mrs. Robinson told Jennyss that she could not sign her name; he asked if he could sign for her. She assented, but, upon further reflection, Jennyss had the doctor/ jailor, Hegemen, sign the letter. When Jennyss tried to get the letters, the order was "protested." Jennyss was never able to get the letters, nor were they ever entered into evidence. What we appear to have is an attempt by Mather, working through Jennyss and Dr. Hegemen, to prevent the letters from reaching the light of day. Through Jennyss, the prosecution had proven a couple of key points. First, that Mather, and, perhaps, Mrs. Robinson had something to hide, and second, that there was some inappropriate connection between Jennyss and Dr. Hegemen.

Beach rose and asked the court if the defense would be permitted to raise issues of medical and legal precedents in the summations without the documents being admitted into evidence. Judge Harris said that the court would allow the use of medical works in closing arguments. Beach, who had been unusually silent during the defense's portion of the trial, announced to the judge that the defense rested.

***

John Upton, a resident of Albany, was placed on the stand by the prosecution to establish that there was intimacy between Mather and Mrs. Robinson. Upton was only allowed to answer a couple of questions before the defense questioned the purpose of his being called. The defense did not want to add too much detail to the stories that were already circulating. The only relevant information that he was allowed to provide was that he knew Mrs. Robinson when she lived in Albany in 1851; however, at that time she was using another name. This line of questioning was followed by a long debate over the need for the prosecution to show the level of contact between Mather and Robinson. Hogeboom expressed his concern that, if he were not allowed to demonstrate that a relationship existed between Mrs. Robinson and Mather, the defense would try to say that her comments about him were another example of her insanity. If allowed to show that Mather was involved with her, this part of her supposed delusion would be nullified.

Harris listened to the argument then stated that he did not

think that it would be possible for the defense to take such a position; therefore, he refused to allow Upton to testify further. When Hogeboom tried to put other witnesses, from Troy, on the stand to testify to the same relationship, this was also denied by Harris.

Oliver Boutwell, who owned the mill near Mrs. Robinson and who lived on the other side of her cottage, was called by the prosecution. This was an interesting choice, since Mrs. Robinson had complained continuously during the spring of 1853, that Boutwell and his family were slandering her. Boutwell was placed on the stand to say that Mrs. Robinson's claim, that the slues way for his mill was causing trouble with navigation, was true and not a figment of her delusions. His testimony was intended to offset the comments that Mrs. Robinson made to Mary Dillon when she said that she had to warn the boat. Boutwell admitted that he was sued for two reasons. First, because boats were pushed onto rocks, and, secondly, a year later, the force of the water had moved the rocks into the channel so that navigation was obstructed, and he was suited again. According to Boutwell, the problem was so serious that, in the spring of 1853, he had to shut down the slues whenever boats wanted to pass.

Peter Cox worked at several jobs, one of which was running a grocery store one block further south of Lanagan's. Cox was placed on the stand to establish the amount and type of alcohol that Mrs. Robinson was drinking during the spring of 1853. The prosecution was banking on showing that her problems were alcohol-related, not insanity. According to Cox, she was in the "occasional habit of getting liquor" at his store. She only drank the best he had, which was usually brandy. When she bought her liquor from Cox, she purchased it by the pint. On a few occasions she purchased a quart of beer, but that was not her habit. Cox's testimony would not have been of much value had it not been for one remark; he said that she "sometimes took a little" swallow while she was still in his store. To drink in public was just not acceptable for a "lady" in Victorian society. Cox acknowledged that, at other times, she just took her drinks with her.

It was on this last point that the true value of Cox's testimony rested. His other job was working on the canal; that meant that he was an employee of Mather. Under cross-examination, the defense tried to show that there was animosity between Cox and Mrs. Robinson. They asked Cox if Mrs. Robinson had ever threatened to have him dismissed. Cox said "No", but, without Mrs. Robinson's testimony, there was no way to be sure.

The defense had used two county employees, Dr. Bontecou and Dr. Hegemen, to document Mrs. Robinson's behavior in jail. The prosecution tried to offset their testimony by placing Franklin Bowman, another deputy, on the stand. Bowman was the only one to testify that Mrs. Robinson acted fairly rational on the night of her arrest. He based his comments on her request to have her clothes brought down to her. It is impossible one hundred and fifty years later to determine the effect of a witness on a jury, but Bowman should have had little or no effect.

When Bowman left the stand, both sides rested. It had been four long days with vastly diverse testimony having been given. Judge Harris called a recess, providing both sides with the night to prepare their closing arguments.

***

It is always interesting to look at a case after it is over and wonder why certain events took place, or to try to guess the reason for the various lawyers' strategies. In this case one major question arises. Why had the defense fought so vehemently to withhold Catherine Lubbee's statement from the jury? The statement is not totally condemning. The entire statement appears in the first section of this book, but the following excerpts deserve closer examination. Although the statement taken in its entirety would have been considered damning, a careful examination of several of Lubbee's remarks might have changed some people's perspective on the case. These are in descending order of importance:

- "I did not see any paper in Mrs. Robinson's hand." This meant that the only witness to the source of the arsenic was Mrs. Lanagan.
- "Mrs. Robinson put about half the sugar in the beer." What happened to the rest of the sugar? Where did it go? The Lanagan's were poor; they never would have wasted half a saucer of sugar. Why was not this sugar tested? Assuming it was poured back into the sugar bowl in the store, what hap-

pened to the arsenic that would have been in there if Mrs. Robinson had, in fact, used the sugar as the vehicle?

- "I never had any words with Mrs. Robinson, nor do I know of any cause of enmity"; also "I never heard that Mrs. Robinson hated Mr. or Mrs. Lanagan." This would have shown once again that Mrs. Robinson had no motive.

- "I saw her put nothing in the sugar or beer except the sugar." These words, even taken literally, take away some of the sting

- "Mrs. Lanagan attempted to remove the floating film off my beer." In her testimony Mrs. Lanagan swore that she tried to take the foam from her own beer, but never mentioned Catherine's. It also raises the question – when did Mrs. Lanagan take the glass away from Catherine, some thing she never mentioned on direct examination.

- "Mrs. Lanagan gave no reason for refusing to drink the beer other than she preferred it without sugar." Mrs. Lanagan had sworn that she no longer liked beer in general, never mentioning the sugar.

Catherine never said clearly that Mrs. Robinson poisoned her, only that she may have had the opportunity.

There was much for the lawyers to think about on the night before closing arguments.

Days 5 & 6

Closing Arguments

During the course of the fifth and sixth days of the trial, there were four key events. These consisted of the closing arguments by the defense and prosecution, each of which were broken into two parts; there was also the summation by the Judge Harris. These three components were all eclipsed, literally, by one awe-inspiring astronomical occurrence that literally stopped the court case.

On the third day of the trial, Judge Harris had been able to coerce Mrs. Robinson into opening her veil and exposing her face, however briefly, to the jury. On the fourth day, she quietly slipped back into her old pattern by wearing a lighter veil than previously. The veil was apparently thin enough not to be offensive; Judge

Harris never commented on it, and it remained as a cover for her face for the entire day. By the fifth day she was back to wearing her heavy blue veil. There were no witnesses who needed to identify her, and she was not asked to remove the heavy shroud.

The defense, being called upon to present their summations first, opted to use the talents of Martin Townsend for their first closing; there would be two. Per the custom of the day, Townsend played the humble servant, apologizing to the jury for his lack of skill, as compared to the eminent counsel for the prosecution. The defense team had planned a methodical presentation that would take five hours to deliver.

Townsend began by explaining that it was the most difficult type of trial for a jury. He reminded the men that it appeared that two innocent people, who felt they were safe in their homes, had died unexpectedly. According to Townsend, this type of act brings out a desire for vengeance in anyone. Therefore, he was required to protect his client and to insure that the jury did not feel the all-too-human pangs of retaliation. It needs to be stressed that Townsend did not say the people were "murdered", leaving that decision to the jury.

Townsend spent a long time talking about insanity as a defense. During this portion of his closing, he stressed two points. First, that insanity did not mean that the individual could not act rationally in some aspects of his life and be insane at others. He also pointed out, repeatedly, that in all of the cases in the county in which the accused had claimed insanity as their defense, there was always a motive for their acts. He stressed that it was a part of the prosecution's responsibility to establish a motive.

Townsend spent some time reviewing cases in New York in which a jury had decided in opposition to what appeared to be overwhelming evidence. He used these cases as examples of why he believed in the jury system. Townsend said he was sure that this jury would be strong and look at the facts, not just the emotional aspects of the case – another reference to a desire for vengeance.

Townsend took time to explain the extraneous aspects of the case that might figure in the jury's decision. He talked about the trial having been postponed three times over the last year, always at the request of the prosecution, although the October postponement was at Pierson's request. He discussed the fact that the Albany newspapers were reporting the political aspects of the case (Townsend was careful to point out that it was not the Troy newspapers, but only those from out of the county that were expressing an opinion that there were people, motivated by the political aspects of the case, rather than a search for justice). He pointed out that the jury should not be swayed by uncertainty about the identity of the person who being tried, a clear reference to the fact that no one knew, for certain, the identity of Mrs. Robinson. Townsend reminded the jurors that it was not her identity that was the question they were asked to decide; it was the issue of the cause of death of Lanagan. Townsend also reminded the jury that this was not a case of morality. Mrs. Robinson's living arrangements, although they may indicate the decline of a woman of culture, were not the issue before the jury. Townsend even tried to deflect the issue of her covered face; he told the jury that her counsel had advised against the ever-present veil, but the veil was not the subject of the trial. Townsend reminded them of her reasons for her persistence in wearing the veil; she had said that it was because she did not want to experience the painful curiosity of the crowd that gathered every day; it was not to mask her face from the expression of emotions.

Townsend then told the jury that, of necessity, he was going to try to speculate on the prosecution's theory. Before he could speculate, however, he asked why, given the fact that Miss Lubbee was a single woman staying with the Lanagan's, why the district attorney had not first examined Mrs. Lanagan as a suspect. Fearing the "sympathy-for-the-grieving-widow syndrome, Townsend told the jury that, although he did not necessarily enjoy doing so, but, if one thought for just few minutes, one could see that Mrs. Lanagan might also have had a motive for murder. He reminded the jury that Mrs. Robinson clearly had none.

Townsend here added an excellent point that had been brought out in the trial, but had not been made a focal point. He stressed that Mrs. Robinson had a history of pulling a handgun from the bodice of her dress when she was angry. If she was angry with one of the victims, and he stressed that no anger had been shown, then why did she choose poison instead of that gun to commit her crime?

Townsend also raised the issue of Mrs. Robinson's failure to try to escape. He reminded the jury that she had gone downtown to shop for furniture instead of fleeing. On the evening of the supposed crime, she had even purchased some products for personal use, hardly the behavior of a person who had just committed a premeditated crime.

One of the problems with having to be first to deliver closing arguments is that it requires anticipation of the other side's positions. Based on the attack launched by the prosecution on the two young doctors, Townsend anticipated that he would need to defend Bontecou and Hegemen. As physicians, they were the best witnesses who had observed Mrs. Robinson. Townsend told the jury that he was sure that the prosecution would attack the young doctors' credibility. He countered with an attack at Hogeboom, reminding the jury that "if he were a resident of the area," he would know the men better "and not take this course."

Townsend then went back to the issue of Mrs. Robinson's insanity, explaining, in his own words, the way the roles of women, men and the values of Victorian Society factored into the equation. In this discussion, Townsend expressed a true understanding of the relationship of Mather and Mrs. Robinson. He pointed out that, because of the clandestine nature of their time together, she did not have the ability to make friends. Her lover became, not only the focus of her being, but the reason for her existence. She was put in a position in which she had only this secretive man to whom to turn for support. He was her link to the world. Townsend's words explain the Victorian expectation, and, to a degree, their perspective of the role of women: "...a woman's fortune is comprised in her affections. She looks at the lover as the one with whom the gratification of ambition, love, respect, and of position and everything that life can furnish is to be consummated." As Townsend reasoned, an unmarried woman had no stature, and a mistress had even less. Townsend pointed out that, as Mather pulled away, she found that she had no one or nowhere to fall back upon; suddenly her life's structure was gone. He discussed her hopes: "She expected to be married – he [Mather] had been absent for some time – she heard he was to marry another – she felt deserted." Townsend at this point acknowledged her background: "she was of a respectable family;

and though she had led a somewhat irregular life, she had hoped that marriage would restore her to a position." Townsend ended this line with a question as to whether God had ever created a woman who would not have gone insane in this situation.

In defense of his client, Townsend attacked Mather and his desire for money and power at the expense of those who cared for him. "He may make money his idol; he may dive into business and secure forgetfulness of the gnawings of a lacerated heart."

Eventually, Townsend even quoted medical sources on the subject of insanity. In these quotes, he drew from the selections that said that even an insane mind had a motive for a criminal act. He returned to the lack of motive on the part of anyone except, perhaps, Mrs. Lanagan. He also used Mrs. Robinson's outbursts in the court as examples of insanity. He said that if the prosecution used alcohol as the reason, rather than insanity, then the jury should ask about the purpose of the alcohol. The conjecture by the jury should be, which came first - the insanity or the alcohol.

Townsend had some fun launching preemptive strikes at the expense of the prosecution. He reminded the jury that, if the prosecution suggested that Hegemen was in some way tainted, why had they not called Sheriff Price? Townsend went on to ask: if the prosecution thought that Mrs. Robinson was sane, why had they not placed a doctor on the stand who would contradict the testimony of Bontecou and Hegemen? At one point, Dr. Adams even examined her (the poison in July), yet the prosecution had not used him to provide testimony about her sanity.

After five long hours, Townsend sat down. He was exhausted, but felt that he had addressed all the major points. Mrs. Robinson leaned over and spoke in a low voice, expressing her opinion of his presentation. "That was all very well said, but it could have all been said in fifteen minutes."

***

In many ways, trial lawyers need the skills of a chess master. They must be prepared for any contingency. They need to dance the fine line between being aggressive for their own clients, but anticipating their opponent's strategy, being prepared to move to a defensive position if required. No matter how clear or just the position of one side, failure to predict the moves of the other could result in the "wrong" decision by the jury.

Since the prosecution is first to present evidence, it needs to anticipate the defense's arguments and to address as many points as possible before the defense starts its opening. In the summations, the defense presents first and must anticipate all of the arguments that will be raised by the prosecution. In every way possible, the defense must try to raise the specter of reasonable doubt concerning the guilt of its client. In this case, the defense put forward an alternative suspect. What Pierson, in the defense's opening, and Townsend, in his summation had done was to suggest that Mrs. Lanagan may have had a motive, something that was never clearly demonstrated for Mrs. Robinson.

There was a lunch break between the presentations of Townsend and of prosecutor Van Santvoord. Shortly after Van Santvoord started his remarks, a nearly total solar eclipse began. It started at 4:22, peaked at 5:29, and ended at 6:37. For nearly one hour, near darkness fell on the city of Troy and on the lives of those gathered in its courthouse. When the dimness was at its deepest point, Van Santvoord sat down silently. A dark spell was passing over the courthouse, and Van Santvoord was going to do nothing to diminish its effects or to allow this act of nature to diffuse his words.

Van Santvoord, in commencing the prosecution's arguments for the jury, said that he and his colleagues had come into this case expecting a defense based solely on the question of Mrs. Robinson's sanity. They never expected that the defense would put forward, "A remote supposition that the act was committed by some other person. He reminded the jury that this [other suspect] was founded, not on proof, but on counsel's inference." Van Santvoord presented an interesting argument regarding the proof that the defense offered regarding a second suspect [Mrs. Lanagan]. In these old trials, the prosecution often worked from the concept that the defense had to prove a different sequence of events from that which was supported through the prosecution's evidence. Van Santvoord, in this case, asked the jury to consider the proof, if any, that the defense offered to portray Mrs. Lanagan as a suspect. He relied on the jury failing to realize that it was not the responsibility of the defense to prove their assertion. The heavy burden of providing proof "beyond a reasonable doubt" falls on the shoulders of the prosecution. The defense only needs to raise the question of reasonable doubt. The prosecution had missed the key play, the possibility that Mrs. Lanagan had committed the murders, and on redirect had not called any witnesses who could have spoken about the positive relationship between the two Lanagans, assuming there were good relations between them.

Van Santvoord argued his position, that of the prosecution, that this was an absolutely straightforward case. In his analysis, Mrs. Robinson had purchased arsenic; this was supported by the fact that a portion of the arsenic was found under her rug. She put something in the drinks, and the people who drank them died as a result. "There cannot be a reasonable doubt as to who committed this crime." He continued, "There is such a thing as moral certainty, as well as mathematical calculation."

Fearing that the jury would have trouble with finding a woman guilty of a crime for which she would hang, Van Santvoord went straight to this issue. "You saw some evidence of the beauty in this woman. You have caught only a glimpse of the countenance that was once beautiful." Having paid a compliment, Van Santvoord went on to turn her looks into a detriment adding, "Do there not lurk, also, the features of violence, profanity, murder?"

On the issue of sanity, Van Santvoord stretched the testimony the farthest. He told the jury that it was not possible to determine a person's sanity in a half-dozen visits, unless the doctor knew the person's behavior before. If one were to accept Van Santvoord's logic, someone who had always acted crazy could never be insane because there had been no change in his behavior. To the prosecution, the observations of Bontecou and Hegemen were just that, observations. Van Santvoord argued that the two doctors did not have the capacity to judge Mrs. Robinson's sanity. Bontecou testified that he had been called upon a dozen times to determine a non-criminal person's sanity.

Van Santvoord discussed the issue of insanity in legal matters. He reminded the jury that insanity was a relatively new defense, and something upon which there was not yet a clear understanding.

There was an irony that added interest to the trial. The irony lay in the introduction of Mather's name to the record. The defense, Mather's allies and friends, had brought out his name. The prosecution, all of whom opposed Mather politically, legally, and ethically, were somehow placed in a position where they could take the moral high road. Van Santvoord had to be lying when he said; "We regret that Mr. Mather's name has been brought into this court in the manner it has been." It was the next comment where Van Santvoord really demonstrated his colors. "There was nothing to show that he had any association with her, whatever." Had Van Santvoord forgotten that fewer than twenty-four hours before his associate Hogeboom had placed Upton on the stand and wanted to call other witnesses specifically to show that there was such an association?

Van Santvoord went on to explain to the jury that Mrs. Robinson had lied to Brownell when she said that she and Mather were married, but it was in his last comment about their relationship that Van Santvoord did his characteristic double talk: "It is not supposed that he (Mather) would correspond with a lunatic, much less that he would live with one." He acknowledged, through his curtness, that Mrs. Robinson was insane.

Van Santvoord enumerated the incidents that the defense witnesses had cited as evidence of insane behavior. He tried his best to explain away each incident. Since some of the stories were hard to explain as sane, he tried to brush these aside. The episode where Mrs. Robinson appeared at Mary Dillon's at 4:30 a.m. in her night-clothes best exemplifies his presentation. He said: "We have no evidence that this conflicts with the character of this woman, when sane." A pause, "She manifested various freaks." He concluded by saying that the incident, "rather agrees with her habits of life and reckless character."

Within Van Santvoord's theory of sanity, Mrs. Robinson's telling Mary Dillon varying stories regarding her past was just one more example of her propensity to lie, not a result of insanity either feigned or real.

As to her agitated behavior on the night she was arrested, Van Santvoord said that the way she acted was natural for someone who had been accused of a capital crime. It is important to note that Van Santvoord did not ascribe her behavior on that night to alcohol.

To the prosecution, the issue was alcohol, not insanity;

Mrs. Robinson was an alcoholic, and the symptoms that she showed on the first two mornings were the results of removal from alcohol (DT's). According to Van Santvoord, Mrs. Robinson's non-reactions toward the two murdered people resulted from her being delirious, not from being insane.

Van Santvoord reminded the jury that a criminal act committed under the influence of alcohol is still a crime. Alcohol is not a mitigating circumstance.

Van Santvoord spoke for more than four hours. Throughout most of his presentation, he took a hard, almost unsympathetic, stand. However, in his last words he provided an indication of his humanity. He cited a recent case in New York City in which the jury found the accused guilty of murder by poison. That same jury had asked the judge to recommend mercy. Van Santvoord faced the jury, looking each man in the eye, as he said, "I have no objection to you following the same course should you see fit." He went on to tell the jurors that, if they were to ask for mercy, in all probability, the court would join in the request to the governor. He had slipped by a call for a "guilty" verdict without appearing to condemn the person to the mandatory death penalty.

After nine hours of presentation, the issues were two. Each juror had to decide in his own mind whether the defense had raised reasonable doubt with the aspersions they had cast at Mrs. Lanagan; if so, the verdict should be "not guilty". If the juror still believed that Mrs. Robinson had committed the crime, then could she, or for that matter could any sane person, kill others with no motive? The jury would not have to answer that question that night, because there were still two more arguments to be heard the next morning.

***

Within moments of beginning his opening remarks the next morning, defense attorney Job Pierson pointed out the same two issues: motive and sanity. Pierson credited himself with a long history of being direct and to the point, that his reputation was based not on making an issue complex, but rather on making it logical and simple.

His next statement indicated that there was substantial disagreement among the defense's team of lawyers, regarding the direction to take in the trial. He openly stated that, "It would appear that the defense thinks it is their duty to convict the prisoner, right or wrong." This split in the defense's theory of the trial was based on the clash of super-egos. Pierson said in his opening remarks that the defense had considered not presenting any witnesses, instead holding firmly to the belief that the prosecution had failed to prove its case. It would appear that Pierson was among those who believed that they should have rested one day earlier.

In his humble opening, Pierson said that through his "fervor, his imagination was gone." Poking fun at himself, he went on, "I might say I never had any." He then, with only a few changes, reargued the same case that Townsend are argued the previous day. He asked the jury to consider whether they believed that any sane murderer would not have fled, let alone return to the scene of the crime. He pointed out that, if one took the prosecution's position that the poisoning occurred at 1:00 p.m., then why would Mrs. Robinson return to the scene an hour and a half later? He also said that it was true that Mrs. Robinson drank, but he pointed out that there was virtually no evidence that she drank to excess, and even less that she was an alcoholic.

Pierson also dwelled at great length on the relationship and testimony of Mary Dillon. He reminded the jury that Mary was a witness with nothing to gain. She saw Mrs. Robinson drink, but not to excess. She saw her cry and dance. Pierson closed this part of his presentation with "Insanity assumes a variety of forms."

Pierson then put on the table an issue that could easily be overlooked one hundred and fifty years later. In November, 1852, Hogeboom ran for Supreme Court Judge in the very court where he was now serving as a visiting prosecutor. The election was close, and there is reason to believe that there were voting irregularities in Rensselaer County; had the irregularities not occurred, Hogeboom would have won the election. There was a perception that Hogeboom was in this trial to clear his reputation; he had lost to a man supported by Mather. Knowing Hogeboom was next, Pierson said, "The gentleman to follow me on the other side, is distinguished as a lawyer, and for his ability and ingenuity of argument. He will attempt to convict the prisoner. He feels his reputation is at stake."

The lawyers for the defense then all took exception to an article that had appeared that morning in the *Whig*. The newspaper maintained that the defense had changed the course of the trial with the testimony of Brownell and by naming Mather. The article made it seem that the defense lacked direction when they entered the trial.

***

In his closing, in which he could speak unabated, Hogeboom proved himself to be the articulate spokesman who had been so widely promoted. He did not present any new arguments; he only added one new theory to those presented by Van Santvoord the day before. He tied the themes together more precisely. Hogeboom built on a thesis; whether it was insanity, her relations with Mather, or her drinking, he was able to take the jury through the issues in a systematic way. He used logic and the power of persuasion to link a case against Mrs. Robinson.

Hogeboom also revisited his implication of witchcraft, or at least spells. He implied that Mrs. Robinson possessed an enchantment over men. To demonstrate her powers, Hogeboom alluded to Hegemen's frequent visits, along with the unrequired visits of Dr. Bontecou and R. C. Jennyss. Through these unnecessary visits, he suggested that there was some secret motivation that caused men to want to be with her. Hogeboom went too far, and named Beach as a victim of her spells. That story was not in the newspaper accounts of the day, probably out of respect for Beach. Years later, in 1894, a lawyer, who was only a clerk at the time of trial, told the story of what happened when Hogeboom mentioned W. A. Beach by name. Hogeboom turned to the jury and asked, "Gentlemen of the jury, do you suppose that Mr. Beach went there to carry this Lucrezia Borgia snuff, knowing him as you do?" Beach's forehead was covered with sweat as he leaped to his feet, demanding an explanation, and an apology. In search of peace, Judge Harris called on Hogeboom to stop this line of elucidation. Hogeboom turned to the jury and almost winked as he said, "Perhaps gentlemen, I do go too far." Beach was red-faced as he sat down. Hogeboom used the incident as a warning to the jury that, if Mrs. Robinson possessed power enough to make a man like Beach act as he had, then, "You must avoid any influence she might exert on you."

In his last two remarks, Hogeboom showed his ability to express himself through the flowery prose of the Victorian Era. "The present is apt to be too powerful upon us. We are more apt to look with mercy upon the living criminal than to turn back and view the dead, stricken down by that criminal." He went on to close, "You have a duty to discharge – a solemn duty. The crisis demands a stern and rigid enforcement of justice. You are the instruments to command the poisoned chalice to the lips of her, who, by administering poison, destroyed the lives of others." Hogeboom returned to his seat. The case against Henrietta Robinson was argued out.

The ultimate decision would soon be in the hands of twelve men, but the case was now in the hands of Judge Harris who called for a brief recess before delivering his charge to the jury.

Harris Charges the Jury

In the 1850's justice was swift. The trial had started with the selection of a jury on Monday afternoon. It was 5:00 p.m. the following Saturday when Judge Harris rose to give his charge to the jury. One of the biggest trials in the country had taken just six days.

It was obvious from Harris's opening remarks that he thought that the penalty for first degree murder might play heavily on the jury. There was only one penalty under the law at that time; a conviction would automatically mean death by hanging. The jurors, when they went in to their deliberations, were not only deciding the guilt of Mrs. Robinson, they would also be determining her fate. To offset the role that the penalty might play in the decision-making process, Harris began by building up the duty of a juror. He spoke about the fact that the obligation for this kind of heavy decision would happen, at most, only once in a person's life. He went on to say that, when it happens, the person needs to make his decision based on the evidence. He spoke about the oath of a juror to render a true verdict, even if it causes the forfeiture of another person's life. Harris then discussed their lives after their decision. He explained that they could only accept themselves if they understood, that through their verdict, they assured that "the laws under which you live and from which we all receive protection, have been faithfully upheld and impartially administered."

Harris continued to address the issue of the death penalty, reminding the jurors that any disagreement with capital punishment belongs with the legislature, not with the court. He made a statement that, if accepted as truth, might change many of the death penalty laws in this country. "The responsibility for taking human life is not upon us but upon the lawgiver."

In his interpretation of the first factual argument, Harris made a tremendous leap. He was discussing the first question that needed to be decided, the cause of death of Timothy Lanagan. Harris said that they had to decide if the poison was administered by the accused. Harris said that, if they, as jurors, believed that the evidence did not support that conclusion, their duty was terminated. To this point, Harris was correct; however, it was his next comment that may have sealed Mrs. Robinson's fate. "But I have not understood the counsel for the defense as contending that the evidence justifies such a conclusion." As Harris heard the case, the defense accepted that Mrs. Robinson had put the poison in the beer. He felt that the defense had not tried to adequately prove that she had not placed the arsenic in the beer. This was a major leap. In fact, Pierson, in his opening, had raised the question of motive. Pierson, in both his opening and closing, had alluded to the possibility that Mrs. Lanagan may have had a motive, but the accused did not. There were only two people still living who were in the room when the poison was ingested. Mrs. Lanagan had taken the stand, and, under the law, Mrs. Robinson could not. How was the defense supposed to contend that Mrs. Robinson was not the perpetrator without one more witness?

On the issue of the poison, Harris drew the conclusion for the jury. Harris stated that Mrs. Robinson was in possession of "the article on which the post mortem" showed was in Lanagan's stomach. Harris reminded the jury that Mrs. Robinson had purchased the arsenic from Ostrom. What had been weakly addressed by the defense was Mrs. Lanagan's assertion that they had no arsenic in their own store. The failure to possess some poison was not logical. The Lanagan's, as store owners, would have needed something to deal with rats and mice. Hygiene in the early Victorian Era was not comparable to that of today. Any store, no matter how clean, if it were within a block of the flour mill and the river, would have had a problem with vermin. Timothy Lanagan would have needed some product to prevent them from destroying his merchandise. The defense should have asked Mrs. Lanagan what product they used in the store to eliminate or prevent pests. She would have to either name a product or admit that they did not take steps to avoid vermin - an answer every farmer on the jury would not have believed.

Harris summarized the story of the fateful day for the jury. Harris retold the incidents, beginning with Mrs. Robinson's arrival in the store at the time the Lanagans and Catherine were having lunch, continuing through the consumption of the beer, ending with the death of Catherine Lubbee at 4:00 the next morning. Harris admitted to the jury, "that this branch of the case depends entirely upon the testimony of Mrs. Lanagan." He went on to point out that, due to the nature of the case, "there could be no other evidence."

What Harris had done with his words was virtually to tell the jury that Mrs. Lanagan was to be believed. He pointed out that "the credibility of Mrs. Lanagan has never been questioned."

Harris nailed the case with his statements, "if her [Mrs. Lanagan's] story is to be believed, it would seem to leave no room for doubt." Effectively, he had said to the jury that they would be fools not to find Mrs. Robinson guilty. He went on to calm any forces of conscience that may hold the jury back. "You cannot hesitate, however painful it may be, to come to the conclusion that it was the accused, and no one else, who administered the arsenic."

The biggest problem with this case was in the way that it was presented. Ultimately, the jury's decision rested completely upon whether or not Mrs. Lanagan was to be believed. There were, after all, only three possible answers. The two most logical, and emotional, were that Mrs. Robinson had placed the poison in the beer, or that Mrs. Lanagan had somehow administered the poison. At the time of this trial there was an exceedingly deep felt axiom that one should never speak ill of the dead. Therefore, the third possibility, although extremely remote, that Catherine had taken her own life and that of her lover rather than to let him live with his wife, was never presented during the trial.

Harris then explained the legal issues of insanity and the use of alcohol. Harris did not bring up temporary insanity, since it would be fifteen years before the concept would be recognized by the American courts. At the time of this trial, the issue was sanity, not temporary insanity. Harris used the standard definition, that if a person realized that what he was doing was a crime and that, as such, he should be punished, he was legally sane. He went on to discuss Mrs. Robinson's use of alcohol. He cited the examples of her purchases both at Lanagan's and at Cox's store. He also told about Ostrom and Brownell saying that they believed she was under the influence of alcohol. The question was, therefore, whether Mrs. Robinson was drunk at the time that she was supposed to have administered the poison. Harris reminded the jury that at 6:00 a.m. Mrs. Robinson purchased a quart of beer and some crackers. Harris said that, since she lived alone, it was reasonable to assume that Mrs. Robinson had consumed the beer herself (In fact, Old-Man-Haley lived in the same house and may have shared the beer). He reminded the jury that she had been in the back room joking with the men, in a very inappropriate manner, at 11:00 a.m. What was never questioned was whether a quart of beer consumed at six in the morning would leave a medium-sized woman still drunk seven hours later. Mrs. Robinson had also eaten at least one potato and an egg before she offered the beer to Mrs. Lanagan and Catherine Lubbee.

In the charge to the jury, it is traditionally left to the judge to explain the issues and the points of law. Rarely does a judge answer the questions that the jury is responsible to answer. Yet Harris continued in his pattern saying, "Upon this state of facts, the question presents itself whether, at the time she committed the fatal deed, the accused was intoxicated." Note that the judge actually said that she had administered the poison!

Harris went on to explain the effect of Mrs. Robinson's possible intoxication on their verdict. "It is my duty to say to you, gentlemen, that if she was intoxicated, even to such an extent that she was unconscious of what she was doing, still the law holds her responsible for the act." Harris had effectively said that, if Mrs. Robinson's insanity manifested itself in drink, it would not be an acceptable defense. To Harris's way of reasoning, the use of alcohol was never a defense.

One of the major precepts of the defense's arguments was the lack of motive for the murders. Defense Attorney Pierson had argued well that, when he was a prosecutor, no person had ever been convicted of a capital crime without a motive being shown. The best that the prosecution could purport as a reason for Mrs. Robinson to use the poison was the failure of Mrs. Lanagan to loan the two dollars that morning. The prosecution had also cited the incident at the dance more than one month before; however, the return of Mrs. Robinson to trading at the store had virtually nullified that motive.

Harris examined the issue of motive from a different perspective than either the prosecution or the defense. He told the jury that there were incidents in which motive could be assumed. He used as his example a hypothetical case in which a person walking down the street pulls out a gun and shoots a second person. He told the jury that, in such a case, the prosecution would not need to prove a motive because "the law without further proof adjudges that it was in his heart to kill him." In this case, the man who pulled the trigger needs to show "affirmatively that he had no such guilty purpose."

Harris went on to make a generalization that, under the law, the voluntary use of alcohol could not be used by the defense as an excuse. He was implying that a person's failure to distinguish right from wrong because of alcohol was not the same as failing to do so because of insanity. He did say that if the "derangement was involuntary and the defendant was no longer capable of discriminating between right and wrong, then the law in its wisdom pronounces him [her] innocent of the crime."

Harris then applied the argument of the use of alcohol to the Robinson case. He said that when a person puts poison in another's drink, even if the reason is that he was "excited by drink," then he must answer to the law. Harris went on to say that "self-inflicted insanity" must not be allowed as a defense; he failed to explain "self-inflicted insanity". He apparently meant that a person could not tell right from wrong because of alcohol.

In examining the charge by Harris to this point, he had resolved every decision for the jury. He had left little, if any, doubt as to who he reasoned to be the person who put the poison in the beer (assuming that it was in the drink). Harris had put the issue of motive aside, saying that it could be assumed, based on the act itself. He elaborated that even the use of alcohol could not be used as an acceptable defense. Because of the way that Harris had explained the case, there was only one issue for the jury to decide, and that was the sanity of Mrs. Robinson.

"If by the visitation of God she was bereft of reason as to be unconscious of the character of the act she was committing, there is an end to her accountability." Those are the words used by Harris to rationalize the issue of sanity; he went on to say that, in the case of sanity, the law assumes that a person is sane, and proof to the contrary is the responsibility of the defense. Here Harris finally said that, "upon this branch of the case, it is your duty to examine the facts in the case with the most diligent care."

Only with respect to the question of sanity did Harris tell the jury they could consider motive. He reminded the jury that the defense had argued that there was no motive for "destroying the lives of Lanagan and Lubbee." Harris acknowledged that absence of a motive always makes the question of sanity "a legitimate subject of enquiry." Harris reminded the jury that, when there was a case based on circumstantial evidence, such as the one being decided in this courtroom, the lack of a motive is "sometimes of vital importance." He again reminded the jury of the fact that in a case in which the accused clearly performed the act, it was not necessary to establish a motive.

Clearly Harris had made all of the decisions for the jury, except with regard to the issue of sanity. It is impossible to put oneself into that courtroom; however, it does not appear from what was printed that Harris was neutral or unbiased.

Harris then took a turn that would be amazing in the light of today's political correctness. He went well past any assumption that insanity rested in the "hand of God." Harris delved into Mrs. Robinson's alleged upper-class background. His words were so moralistic that they need to be reported exactly as he is quoted to have said them; the words also should be viewed as an example of the way the parties saw each other: "If it be true, as has been assumed throughout the trial, that the accused is of gentle birth, and has once moved in the higher and more refined walks of life, what a painful illustration she presents of the rapid descent which a woman makes to the lowest depths of degradation and vice, when she once consents to take leave of virtue and innocence. We have this fallen woman, who is described to us as possessing high accomplishment and lady-like manners, voluntarily mingling with the parties at the grocery-dance." Note that Harris indirectly demeaned the Lanagans and their neighbors calling them "the parties" at the dance. Harris went on to characterize the altercation with Smith as a "brawl".

Throughout his closing argument, Harris continually weighted his presentation to the side of the prosecution. He seemed to dismiss the loan argument, but refocused the jury's attention on the dance and on the altercation between Mrs. Robinson and Mrs. Lanagan that occurred a couple of days later. He reviewed the incident for the jury claiming that Mrs. Robinson's pride had been injured. Harris reminded the jury that, according to the prosecution, it was this incident that had "left a sting rankling in her bosom … which needed the excitement of which she was the subject on the 25 of May, to arouse to such a degree as to make resolve upon the destruction of those who had become the subjects of her resentment." Harris made it clear that this argument would be acceptable, although weak, as a reason for someone in "sound mind." Harris seemed to make it clear that Mrs. Robinson was not of sound mind, characterizing her as being of "irascible temperament" and, at the time of the commission of the crime, excited by stimulants and "other vitiating (morally corrupt) causes."

Harris reopened the issue of her sanity, reminding the jury of the impressions of Mary Dillon and Anthony Goodspeed. In a further example of Harris's perception of the "new Americans", he called Mary Dillon "artless …with a taste for romance." Harris said that Mrs. Robinson was forced into a situation that "compelled her to live alone," but that, out of loneliness, she associated with people who had "no tastes or sympathies with her own."

Harris reminded the jury of the difference between those behaviors that might be considered insane before the incident and those after. Those before the incident were legitimate to consider, while those after the arrest could be heavily influenced by the understanding of the charges and their possible ramifications.

In one of the strongest points that he made on behalf of the defense, Harris reminded the jury that two physicians who met with Mrs. Robinson after her arrest thought that she was "not rational." He did remind the jury that the physicians' observations were made while she was in jail charged with a capital crime and should be considered in that context. Harris acknowledged to the jury that while she was in jail Mrs. Robinson's behavior was "indeed strange." Harris said that the withdrawal of stimulants could have been one the reasons for Mrs. Robinson acting out in the jail.

"Here my duty ends and yours begins," stated Judge Harris as he was bringing to an end his charge to the jury. He characterized his performance as "imperfect" (the use of humility was common in the closing of judges as well as lawyers); he characterized himself as having the "single aim" to discharge his responsibilities as a judge with a "steady and unswerving hand." In his final words to the jury, Harris was the most neutral and compassionate. He said, "In the discharge of your duty, be faithful to your own obligations. Deal justly with this poor, unhappy woman, whose destiny is now committed to your hands. Deal mercifully with her too. This is your privilege. The law allows every grounded doubt to avail for her acquittal. If, after a full consideration of the facts in the case, no such doubt rests upon your mind, you must not hesitate, though it be with anguish of heart, to pronounce her guilty. But if you can, after all, say that you are not satisfied with her guilt, it will be your agreeable duty to pronounce a verdict of acquittal."

Harris had also shown himself to be a man of his times. His arguments and his characterization of the accused are filled with the values of Victorian society. The Victorian Era, which is so highly espoused today, was actually a very unforgiving period. It was an age rooted in extremes; there was "good" and there was "evil", but there was little or no forgiveness for mistakes. To be truly "good", people had to take care of those who were not (thus the major role of charity during this period). Those who were not "good" were never to be taken into the inner circle of society. Harris had used his courtroom as a preacher uses his pulpit. He had subtly degenerated the Lanagans, belittling their dance, while intimating that we should be accepting of them, as if they would know no better. He had used the term "rowdies" to describe the men in the back room of the grocery; he had used Mrs. Robinson as an example to young women of the plight of those who made even one bad choice. Harris had, on this afternoon, exposed his personal values and those of the Victorian inner circle.

Apparently Harris thought it was an exceptionally good closing. Harris often boasted that it was published in Justice Parker's criminal reports as an example in a charge for an insanity case.

It would be interesting to know how Judge Harris thought the jury would find in the case. There is no record that he ever stated what rendering he believed the jury should have made, but we can assume that, since he was one of the people who called on Wilson to write the book, he believed the arguments he presented were correct, if not the verdict. His closing remarks give the impression that he believed she was guilty but that the reason was insanity.

The reports in the newspapers said that the people who attended the trial felt that there would be a hung jury. The newspapers did not think that the jury would be held up by her guilt or innocence; they thought that the conflict within the jury would stem from the issue of sanity. The newspapers theorized that the insanity argument was too pervasive and too controversial in this case for humble farmers to reach an agreement.

Harris was complimented by the *Troy Times* for his handling of the case. The newspaper said that his decisions regarding the admissibility of evidence and the issue of Mrs. Robinson's refusal to remove her veil were handled with respect for the law. In their opinion, he had shown himself to be a gentleman worthy of the position he held. In his decision during the trial, the judge did show himself to be balanced and professional; it was in his charge to the jury that he was very direct and opinionated.

At 6:30 the jury retired to make its decision. After the jury left the room, Judge Harris called for a recess. Even though it was the dinner hour, there was no rush to leave the building. Many stayed and mingled for some time.

Mrs. Robinson, in the care of Sheriff Price and his daughter, was taken back to the jail in a carriage. The carriage was probably used as a precaution. There was, at the time, the potential for people to become overly enthusiastic in their efforts to see Mrs. Robinson.

Verdict

&

Beyond

Verdict

It was almost 9:00 p.m. that evening when Judge Harris resumed his place on the bench. The courthouse bell had rung a few minutes earlier, signifying that the jury had reached a decision. Harris knew that there was only one decision, in a case of this magnitude, that could be reached this quickly. He sat on the bench, holding his head in his hands. People in attendance could see that this man, a mighty oak, had been moved to tears.

Throughout her trial, Mrs. Robinson had the best counsel available in Troy. She had continually expressed to Price that she thought that there would either be acquittal or, at the very worst, there would be a hung jury. In Wilson's book, he provides the following account of the trip to the sentencing; this report could not be found in any other source. The account tells of her mood and gives some indication of her family. Now, with her fate being decided, she showed some signs of weakening. She turned to Price and asked, "Do your think the verdict will be against me?"

Price, well-experienced in the meaning of such a quick verdict, told her that he could not provide any encouragement. He went on to say, "I fear it will be so."

Now, understanding the full force of the crisis that had become her life, she said in a low voice, "Oh! That my brother William was here. Oh! That I could see my brother, William."

Price was certain of what he had heard, but he wanted her to repeat it one more time; he asked, "What did you say about your brother, William?"

"Nothing of consequence; I was merely thinking." With those words, she settled back into the role of the silent witness to her life.

***

By the time the carriage from the jail arrived at the courthouse, a throng of people had gathered to hear the verdict. There were so many assembled that some people were forced to remain out in the street in front of the building. There was little street lighting at the time, so, as soon the sun was fully down, it was considered "late". Regardless of the hazards of the night, a full one-third of the people who had made their way into the courtroom were women. Sheriff Price, his wife, and daughter realized the peril of trying to use the front entrance. They elected to convey Mrs. Robinson into the court through the back door.

To the crowd that was drawn together to witness history, there was no perceptible difference in Mrs. Robinson. As she had done throughout the trial, she remained closely veiled, her features protected by one of her blue shrouds. At least in her own mind, she was a woman of prominence, and, as such, she walked into the room erect, almost strutting. She was, as always, fashionably dressed.

Even before the jury walked into the room, the emotions were so intense that they could literally be sensed. It was as if the room had developed its own energy. When the jury finally entered, they did not face Mrs. Robinson; not looking at the defendant was considered to be a clear sign of the verdict. As they walked to their assigned seats, the jurors' faces were all turned toward the floor. Tears could be seen in the eyes of several of the men on the jury.

It took a long time for the room to finally become quiet. However, when the proceedings started, the room was absolutely silent, each person intent on what was transpiring. Eventually the clerk spoke, "Gentlemen have you reached a verdict?"

After a minute's pause, the foreman, Alison Cook (male), answered, "We have." The very utterance of the words ate at him so severely that he had to lean forward, his face buried in his handkerchief.

The clerk turned to Mrs. Robinson and said, "Prisoner look upon the jury." He then turned to the jury and said, "Jury, look upon the prisoner." He paused for only a moment before he uttered the next words in his well-rehearsed speech. Still looking at the jury, he said, "You say you have agreed on a verdict. Do you find the prisoner 'guilty' or 'not guilty'?"

Rare are the moments when the courtroom in Rensselaer County was ever as quiet as it was during the ensuing pause; not one person gathered was willing to miss hearing the next word that was expected. Finally, the foreman responded, "Guilty!"

The room remained silent except for the clamor of the few who immediately left the room to spread the word to those who were not present to witness the proclamation for themselves.

The clerk continued, "Prisoner, hearken unto the verdict, as recorded by the court." Turning his attention back to the jury, the clerk said, "You say you find the prisoner guilty of the murder wherewith she stands charged. So you all say?"

At that time, Pierson stood and asked that the jury be polled. It was a normal demand. Harris had no trouble accepting the request and ordered the jury to be polled. When each member's name was called, he responded in various tones, "guilty".

District Attorney Anson Bingham, who had been more of a witness to the trial than a participant, asked that the court proceed with the sentencing.

Job Pierson rose and was asking the court to suspend the sentencing when suddenly Mrs. Robinson stood up and started shouting. "Shame on you Judge! Shame on you! There is corruption here! There is corruption in the court!", Mrs. Robinson continued her harangue, despite the efforts of Sheriff Price, his wife, and daughter to calm her.

At first, Pierson tried to help to quiet Mrs. Robinson, then he gave up and turned to the judge, asking for a postponement of the sentencing until, at least, Monday. Over Mrs. Robinson's uproar, Pierson said that the defense had some legal arguments that needed to be made prior to the sentencing. Pierson was referring to what he believed was a lack of legal notice given by the Grand Jury. As Mrs. Robinson sat down, Pierson could be heard to say that the defense would be able to argue the issue on Monday, if the court would assent to a recess until that time.

Before Harris could make his ruling on the temporary adjournment, Mrs. Robinson was back on her feet. In a voice that carried throughout the courtroom, she screamed, "The court is corrupt! There is corruption in the district attorney's office! Some of the jurors are corrupt! I demand another judge!" The quality of her voice was somewhat shrill as she repeated her assertions that there was corruption throughout the system. Although it was unconventional, she did show that she could enunciate her words clearly, the sign of a formal education.

Exasperated at trying to maintain decorum in the place he respected the most, Pierson turned to Mrs. Robinson and said, "If you do not keep quiet, I will leave you."

His words were like trying to put out a fire by using gasoline. "I will speak! Why should I not?", was her booming answer.

In the middle of the fray, Martin Townsend rose; he was as heated as Mrs. Robinson, but not for the same reasons. He turned to the judge and exclaimed, "In finding a verdict of guilty, this jury has convicted the veriest lunatic that ever lived." At that exact moment there were many in the court who probably would have agreed with Townsend's assessment. Along with his associate, he asked for a postponement until Monday. Pierson and Townsend told the judge that they needed time to consult.

It took a while for the sheriff and his family to get Mrs. Robinson to sit down and to be quiet. When she finally took her seat, she became silent, like a child who is accustomed to pouting when she has been sent to her room.

Through the excitement that permeated the room, Harris announced that he doubted that a postponement until Monday would prejudice the case. The problem was that Harris was scheduled to hear another case in Catskill on Monday. He reflected for a few moments, then added that he "felt bound by the wishes of counsel."

In an effort to be done with the highly-charged sentencing, Hogeboom, based on his understanding of the points raised by Pierson, said, "As for the people, we see no reason why the issues raised by the defense cannot be raised after sentencing."

Harris ruled wisely, saying, "I feel it is my duty to conform to the wishes of the prisoner's counsel." He barely paused before he called out, "Court is adjourned until 8:30 Monday."

Mrs. Robinson led the way as she, Sheriff Price, his wife, and daughter proceeded out the front doors. According to most sources, Mrs. Robinson made her way through the crowd with her usual strong, forceful step. When the entourage descended the steps of the courthouse, there was a carriage waiting. The four rode the five blocks back to the jail in what could only be considered a surreal episode.

One newspaper said that Mrs. Robinson was emotionally weakened by the decision and needed assistance into the carriage. It mattered little whether she needed help into the carriage; she had set the criterion by walking out the front. Even in defeat, she was not one who would slink out through the back door.

Over the weekend, a description became public of that remarkable carriage trip back to the jail. Mrs. Robinson had spent the ride laughing and joking with Price and his family, as if what had just happened in the courtroom was a scene out of a play rather than the decision of a tribunal. During the short ride, she talked incessantly about the scene in the courtroom. According to Wilson, when she got to her cell, she turned to her jailer and said, "You'll have a good time putting a rope around my neck, old boy!"

If her life were a play, Henrietta Robinson had finally lost control of the script.

Sunday

On Sunday, those in the jail suffered under their own cloud of stress. Everyone knew the sentence; after all, there was only one. The judge had no options; the penalty for murder in the first degree was death by hanging. Having the sentence held in abeyance did not change the outcome; it only postponed the inevitable. This Sunday was one more example of the fact that it is almost always worse to wait for news than to hear it immediately.

When Price brought Mrs. Robinson her breakfast, he found her dressed completely in spotless white. If there were one day in her life when white was inappropriate, it was this Sunday. Mrs. Robinson paced her cell for most of the day, alternating between two diametrically opposing moods. At times she called for vengeance against the prosecuting team, the judge and any others whom she felt had in some way contributed to her downfall; at other times, she could be heard vengefully saying over and over, "He shall never pass sentence against me! No, never! Never! Never!" Minutes later, she would be joking and full of merriment. After one particularly robust burst of anger, she became a truly Victorian lady and fainted from exhaustion.

The cycle of emotions was so blatant that Price called for a watch to be placed on her so that she did not commit suicide. It is odd, when a rational examination is made, that, in jails, people are protected from ending their own lives so that society can take them from them later.

Monday

At 8:20 in the morning, the judges had not yet taken their seats when Mrs. Robinson returned to the courtroom. It was a work day, yet the room was filled beyond capacity. Like moths to a flame, people were attracted to the court house by the potential for electrifying excitement. Stories had circulated throughout the city about her behavior, both at the time of the verdict and in the jail on Sunday. For the overflow crowd that was at the courthouse, there was no reason to believe that there was any less promise of excitement on this day.

Mrs. Robinson was expressing the full range of emotions by the colors she chose to wear. The day before, she had worn virginal white as she called down curses upon those whom she considered to have wronged her. Today, she was dressed in a black silk dress; one might have expected her demeanor to be even more bizarre. On this day, it appeared as if she had dressed for a wake. The only white she wore was her hat, but even that was covered by the familiar dark blue veil. As always, when in public, she was perfectly groomed.

There was not sufficient standing room, and certainly not enough seats, for everyone who wanted admission. The crowd was so large that the second floor balcony was actually seen to sag from the weight. One of the more atypical aspects of those in attendance was that over half of the people were women. The women, many of whom had brought their children with them, were seen to stand on the benches to get a better view of the Veiled Murderess. Parents of both genders held their children high so that they might glimpse the woman who had become a local celebrity. People in overcrowded conditions universally tend to become restless. The court room on this day was no exception. The enthusiasm of those in the room was demonstrated by anxious words and short tempers. It was early in the day, but the heat of so many bodies, combined with lack of fresh air, caused several of the ladies in the gallery to faint. As they were carried outside, others took their places.

At exactly 8:30 a.m., the three judges entered the room. As presiding judge, Harris entered last. Try as hard as they could, the officers of the court were unable to secure the silence that Harris was seeking. There was a constant turbulence in the audience.

Those who had come intent on getting a glimpse of the prisoner were naturally disappointed; this day, as in all others, the veil covered Mrs. Robinson's face so completely that her features were barely visible; certainly no expression of emotion could be seen.

Harris tried once more to secure silence, calling on those present to "feel it incumbent…to preserve order." Realizing that true order was never to be obtained, Harris motioned to Beach to begin his statement. His words were exactly what those gathered did not want to hear. Beach asked Harris to suspend sentencing until further deliberations with his counselors could be held. Beach's claim was based on two very different issues. The first was a highly technical issue related to the appointment of the Grand Jury which had issued the indictment. Beach may have been correct, but the issue was not exciting. Although he did state at least one case in which, based on the same situation, a retrial had been ordered, those in the audience wanted action, not legal issues. The second reason for Beach's desire to have a postponement was much more compelling. Beach claimed that one of the jurors had been heard to say prior to the trial that he was certain that Mrs. Robinson was guilty. When that same man had been questioned by the court before his selection, he claimed that he had no opinion regarding her guilt.

Hogeboom objected, noting that any appeals could be made after the sentence had been passed; therefore, any delay was unwarranted. He put forward the prosecution's argument that any question about the Grand Jury should have been raised before the trial, not after. With respect to the juror, Hogeboom said that the defense had selected the jury, going so far as to say, "It was the defense's jury." This argument, although appealing, was really not relevant to the issue of a juror who had misrepresented himself.

The sides continued their arguments for several minutes. Harris listened patiently, as he had throughout the trial. The judge ultimately ruled in favor of the defense, noting that it was in the spirit of the law that all deliberations should be permitted. He went on to say that he would not make any comment intimating his opinion on the sentencing. This decision was based on his own feelings, not on any restriction from the law, as the verdict had already been reached.

Upon hearing that no sentence was to be handed down that day, the crowd became energized. They had come for a show, not for an intermission. To make the situation even worse, Mrs. Robinson gave no overt demonstration of emotion. The most exciting thing that happened was the women fainting in the gallery.

Realizing that Harris was not going to be swayed in postponing the sentence, Bingham asked the court if there were to be any change in the guard of the prisoner. The underlying question did not refer to her confinement within the jail, but whether she were to remain in jail or go to one of the state's prisons. Her lifestyle would change immeasurably for the worse if she were to be held in a prison.

Harris responded, "Her guard is to remain as heretofore, unless otherwise ordered by the court."

Mrs. Robinson was to remain as a guest of the county. Her cell would continue to be full of her personal possessions. She would dress in her own clothes and continue in the lifestyle to which she had become accustomed during the previous year.

***

It was one week before the *Albany Morning Express* put a social "spin" on those who attended the trial that had consumed the Capital Region's interest. The article was evocative of the social moralizing that newspapers articulated throughout the Victorian Era. The *Express* acknowledged that any murder trial created a morbid curiosity. The editor declared the belief that, in the trial of Mrs. Robinson, women of good character should not have listened to the facts, since many were "of a revolting character, and showed her (Mrs. Robinson) to be one of the most degraded of her sex." Yet the newspaper recognized that each day one hundred or more women gathered in the courtroom. What made the problem even more distasteful for the *Express,* was the fact that, the more demeaning the facts, the stronger the women in the audience clung to their seats. In the strong fatherly mold that fit so many newspaper editors of the era, they scolded the community saying that, by attending and hearing 'every new fact brought out against the poor victim of passion and depravity who was on trial for her life," these women had brought shame to their gender. The editor went on to express the newspaper's values saying, "For our own part we would never witness such sad and sickening spectacles if our duty did not compel us to do so."

The editor was none other than the little dictator himself, Thurlow Weed.

***

Wilson relates one story which makes it doubtful that, by the time of these articles, Sheriff Price would hold Mrs. Robinson and her cause in high esteem. After her conviction, Mrs. Robinson started to blame all of her problems on Price and his family; she was suddenly sure that they were out to destroy her. It is worthy of note that, under the law, Price or one of his deputies would have become her executioner; she may have believed that the family was trying to expedite the process. One morning in the early part of July, 1854, as Price brought Mrs. Robinson her breakfast, she grabbed a marble-bottomed candle stick and used it to hit Price in the forehead. The blow was totally unanticipated and, according to Price, unprovoked. The blow literally leveled the sheriff, and the bruise that resulted became an ugly presence on his face. Getting control of the situation, Price ordered her cuffed and chained. It took several days for her to calm down enough that Price thought she could be trusted to behave in the cell without restraints.

Who Was Mrs. Robinson
Part II

The furor over the true identity of Mrs. Robinson re-emerged on the third day of the trial. Speculation had never really been absent, but rumors began in earnest when Judge Harris insisted on that morning that she remove her veil. She had refused, understanding that in so doing she would have to accept any ramifications, claiming that she would choose consequences over becoming a spectacle. Later, she was compelled to briefly remove the veil.

The *Troy Whig* used the incident as a door that, having been opened, allowed them to comment on her overall conduct during the trial. The behavior they stressed was her insistence on keeping her real name a secret. Nestled in the middle of the commentary were two paragraphs that pointed out the public's general perspective on her identity. The paragraphs which commented on her identity resulted in a series of articles that were meant to settle the issue. Instead they raised the public's interest to a new level.

These paragraphs read:

> It may not be improper to say that the current belief is – not to use a stronger term - that Mrs. Robinson, the prisoner, formerly – some twenty years ago – resided in this city, as a pupil at the Seminary; that her family was one of wealth, standing and respectability – and resided somewhere near Quebec; that while here she moved in the best circles of our city, as did her three sisters who also attended the Seminary at different times; that she subsequently married an army officer in Canada, who died; that she then married a surgeon in the army, in the Provinces, from whom she separated; and that she is now here, the veiled prisoner at the bar, charged with the crime of murder.
>
> These, we believe are the outlines of the narrative generally credited – we may say not doubted from the first – by very many. For what reason her identity has been attempted to be disguised, we do not know. Shortly after the prisoner was arrested, a gentleman from Quebec or vicinity came here; and a statement was put forth to the effect that the prisoner was some other person; but it is now to be presumed that the representation is not sustained in the public belief. Whoever the prisoner is, she has from the first possessed the facilities for securing for herself the ablest counsel, and many comforts not possessed by all who inhabit a cell.

The article went on to describe both Mrs. Robinson's behavior and her dress each day. It was one of the few times in the history of Troy in which the dress of a person on trial made such a fashion statement. The article also hypothesized on the effect that the veil was having on the public's awareness of the case. The *Whig* reasoned that the veil actually increased interest. The article closed with, "it is difficult to say; but true that the drama, as cast, excites a deep interest."

The last comment could be considered as a prophecy because it resulted in a series of articles that were read by everyone interested in the case. Within a day, the Albany newspapers were quoting the *Whig*'s article. Ultimately, it was reprinted in several of the local newspapers; each time the *Whig* was credited.

The *Whig* and *Troy Daily Times* were rival newspapers, both trying to increase their circulation by being the first to break a story about the murders. The Whig had won by stressing the veil. Four days later the *Times* finally joined in the identification race by agreeing with the *Whig's* finding, that Mrs. Robinson was indeed one of the Wood sisters, but adding a new detail, saying that she had been recognized in the courtroom by one of her classmates from the Seminary. The *Times* had taken the story from speculation to identification. The *Times* reported that, on the third day, in the court room, a conversation had taken place between Mrs. Robinson and one of her former classmates. The *Times* had an interesting description of the proceedings in general. They felt that the entire trial had turned into an event "more like a romance than reality."

In early June of 1854, less than a month after the jury had rendered its verdict, two letters addressing the question of her identity appeared in the same issue of the *Whig*. The first letter was from Mr. Willard, the husband of Emma Willard, head of the Seminary. The second letter was from William Wood, the presumed brother of Mrs. Robinson. Both letters refuted the conjecture that Mrs. Robinson was one of the Wood sisters. The letters were sent to the editor of the *Whig* with the understanding that they were to be published in their entirety. In fact, Wood made it very clear that he expected his letter to be printed; he wrote, at the end of his letter, "papers which have published an account of the trial of Henrietta Robinson will oblige by giving the above insertion." The letters are important enough in the pursuit for her identity, even today, to include in their entirety.

The letter of J.H. Willard reads as follows:

Sir: I received the enclosed communication for you this morning, and in connection with it I should like to say a few words. It is well known to my friends that I do not believe that Mrs. Robinson is in any way related to the family of the Woods, or that she was ever connected with the Seminary. For some circumstances which have come to my knowledge, I suppose her to be Mrs. Campbell, (this, I think, is the name, though I am not positive) who was a native of Quebec, from a respectable family there, and who resided in the vicinity of Mr. Wood at the time his daughters were in Troy, and who knew of their being here. She married, but soon lost her husband. She, not long after, went to

Mr. Wood to ask for assistance to go to Scotland to visit her husband's relatives. Mr. Wood gave her nearly fifty dollars, which sum was expended in Quebec instead of using it for the purpose for which it was obtained. She afterwards went again to Mr. W. for more money, which he, not being satisfied with the disposition made of the first, declined giving. She very soon after set up a drinking house in the suburbs of the city, and while there, persuaded a young man of respectable connections in Quebec to elope with her to New York. This is the last that is known of her. The young man was said to have been seen there as a cab driver. Now, if Mrs. Robinson is this Mrs. Campbell, it is not at all difficult to see how she obtained the knowledge of many of the circumstances of which she made use in persuading those who have been about her, that she was a member of the Wood family. Her knowledge of the persons belonging to the families in which she professed to have visited could very readily have been acquired during the several months residence in this city previous to her arrest, and having the object in view of passing for the person she is assumed to be, it is not to be supposed that she would neglect the use of any means which would aid her in the accomplishment of that end. This supposition will easily account for her recognition of a lady whom she addressed in court by her family name, the lady having been married for several years. Among other circumstances tending to show conclusively that Mrs. Robinson is not one of the Woods, is a remark made to me by Mr. Beach, one of her counsel, very soon after his first interview with her. "I expected," said he, "to have found at least traces of education and refinement in her, but in a conversation of half an hour, I found neither."

Mr. Jeffreys, the gentleman from Quebec, whose testimony is so much relied upon as proving the identity of Mrs. Robinson with Miss Wood, did not even see her while he was in Troy, and has recently written to a gentleman of this city, stating that he has, since his return, seen letters from all the daughters of Mr. Wood, written within a short time past.

Another strong point is the fact that Mr. William C. Heart, who was in my office as bookkeeper during the time that the Misses Wood were members of the Seminary, and who was necessarily perfectly familiar with their appearance, saw Mrs. Robinson repeatedly in the Bank, of which he is a teller, and in the street, and though very much impressed by her English or

Canadian look, still never thought, and is now quite certain from his recollection, that she cannot be either of them, and finally we have the word of a gentleman, Mr. W. P. Wood, whose character is unimpeached and unimpeachable, against that of a woman who has for one year been leading a life of shameless profligacy. Mr. Wood was in Troy last summer, almost immediately after the arrest of Mrs. Robinson, and at that time furnished the names and residences of his sisters, all or whom had been seen by him at their residences in Great Britain within three months previous to the time he was here, and which are as follows:

Georgianna, the eldest, is living in London. She is the widow of William Capel Clayton, the eldest son of Sir William Robert Clayton, Bart, of Harleywood, Marlow, England.

Emma, the second, is the wife of Dr. McIntosh, recently surgeon of the Royal Artillery, son of the late celebrated Dr. McIntosh of Edinburgh and she is now living in Scotland.

Charlotte, the third daughter, is married to the eldest son of Sir William Francis Elliott, Bart., of Stob's Castle, Roxburgshire, Scotland, in which country she and her husband reside.

Harriet, the fourth daughter, resides in Dublin, with her husband, Capt. Mackay, of the Royal Artillery, who is now stationed in that city. Capt. Mackay is the son of the late Col. Mackay of Bighouse, Scotland.

Maria, the youngest daughter, who was never at the Seminary, is now residing with her sister, Mrs. McIntosh.

It is said that Mr. Wood might be influenced by a desire to cover the disgrace to his family, from the conduct of an unworthy member, and therefore would be led to make a false statement with regard to it.

When Mr. Wood was here, he went with me to the jail in order, if possible to see Mrs. Robinson. Now, if I know anything of the manifestation of human feelings in the manner and in the countenance, I know that that man never could have gone to the prison of a sister under charge of a most cold blooded and deliberate murder, as he went with me at that time.

When we reached her room, the Sheriff opened her door, so as to give us an opportunity of seeing her as she lay upon her bed. She was so covered that we saw only the upper parts of her face and her hand. From the size and appearance of the hand and wrist, I was more fully confirmed in my opinion, if possible, than I had been before. She as usual – and as she has done two or three times by Mrs. Willard and myself – refused to see us.

She recognized Mr. Wood, as was to be expected, from her former residence near his father's.

She said then, very much as she had done when I called before to see her, that she had no brother, and *she was not the person we supposed*, meaning evidently that she was not Miss Wood – and refusing what would have been a certain means of identifying herself if she were what she professed to be.

I should have made these statements before, but was in Virginia during the trial of Mrs. Robinson, and since my return have been so much occupied that I have not until now found the time to prepare it.

J. H. Willard

The letter written by Willard raises numerous questions. It probably raised more questions than it was hoped to answer. To start, one has to wonder why Willard had even written the letter? What could have been his motives – to help a friend? Perhaps to protect the name of the Seminary? If his motive was to stop the rumors, the letter was a failure. Some of the questions raised because of the text are:

How could Willard expect anyone to believe that he could identify a former student by looking only at her wrist?

Willard's explanation of the incident in which she was recognized by her classmate and called by her family name instead of her assumed name is totally reversed. How would her "stay of several months" have provided her classmate with her birth name when she had been living under the name Mrs. Robinson?

How did Willard obtain the name "Mrs. Campbell", if not through Mr. Wood? If it were through Wood, why did not Wood himself put the name forward? Was Wood using Willard's name and status in Troy to defuse the assault on his family?

If they wanted to prove that Mrs. Robinson was really the Mrs. Campbell named in the letter, why had not an effort been made to find Mrs. Campbell through the "young man" who was working as a cab driver in New York City?

Willard claims to quote a comment made by Beach about Mrs. Robinson. This comment was made after Beach's first visit with her in jail. This was in the period that virtually all the witnesses, both those for the defense and those for the prosecution, said that she acted irrationally. In the quotes of Beach, why had Willard not obtained a letter from him rather than use a quote?

Willard characterizes his former business manager, Heart, as saying that at first, he did not think that the woman who came to his bank was one of the Wood girls, but now he was sure it was not. It had been eight years and a myriad of life experiences since the Wood girls were at the Seminary; might their appearances have changed? Again, as in the quote of Beach, why had Willard not obtained a letter from Heart rather than quote him?

Willard states that Wood could not have gone to the jail with him if he had believed he was on his way to see his sister. Why not? Was he the type that would disown a sister for embarrassing the family?

There are two possible explanations as to why the woman in jail was referred to as Miss Wood, and, as Willard said, she was not the person whom people supposed her to be. It would have been honest to deny that the lady in jail was a Wood because, if she had married, she would no longer have been a "Miss Wood". Finally, we need to understand that at the time the speculation was that this was Emma Wood. What if she were one of the other sisters?

***

The second letter, published immediately after the one from Mr. Willard, was from Mrs. Robinson's supposed brother, William.

Sir: - having seen an article in the *Troy Daily Whig* of the 25th of May, relative to the trial of Henrietta Robinson, wherein it is stated: - [At this point the first paragraph from the article, wherein the *Whig* had stated that the veiled prisoner was one of the Wood family, was quoted in full.]

Being a member of the only family residing in or near Quebec of the name answering to the above description, I feel myself compelled to deny that this Henrietta Robinson is in any way whatever connected with my family. I had four sisters, pupils at Mr. Willard's Seminary. All of whom are now residing in Great Britain – One of them married an officer of the British army in Canada, and after his death married in Quebec, Doctor MacIntosh of the Royal Artillery, with whom she is now living in Assynot House, Granton, Ross shire, Scotland

W. F. Wood

154

***

The publication of these letters on Thursday failed to halt the rumors that, by this time, had become virtually irrepressible. If anything, the letters added fuel to the fodder that powered the rumor machine. There had been gossip that one of the Wood sisters had married twice, once to a soldier and once to nobility. This profile matched what had been in the newspaper regarding the second eldest sister, Emma.

There is a side tale that Wilson learned concerning Mr. Wood's visit to the jail. It seems that, when Wood came to the door of the jail, Sheriff Price's little daughter answered. Without being introduced, the daughter went to get her mother, saying, "Mrs. Robinson's brother is here." This observation was based on a little girl's recognition of how much the two people looked alike.

The *Whig* did not say why it was suddenly attempting to defend the Wood family, but on the Saturday following the publication of the letters from Willard and Wood, a reporter from the *Whig* actually met with William Wood, the brother and author of one of the letters. Wood provided a series of four letters from his sisters who were residing in Great Britain (there was no letter from Harriet who was in Ireland). All of the letters were in their original envelopes and carried a foreign postage mark. In an obvious effort to dispel the concept that Mrs. Robinson was Emma, there were two additional letters regarding that one sister. In addition to a letter said to be in Mrs. McIntosh's own hand, there were letters from Wood's youngest sister, Maria, who resided with Emma. The last was from Emma's daughter, in which she mentioned her mother.

By the time of the trial, the parents of William Wood had passed away. The father's estate was managed by a lawyer in Quebec; that lawyer provided Mr. Wood with an affidavit that stated that he was regularly in touch with Emma, as he was required to provide her with payments on a monthly basis. The lawyer swore before a notary that Emma had not left Great Britain since her move there in 1849.

When this letter was printed, the location of the meeting between the *Whig* reporter and Mr. Wood was unclear. The affidavit that the lawyer provided was dated June 9, the same day that the letters were published in Troy. The problem is that the *Whig*'s meeting with Wood happened two days later; therefore, Wood could have come to Troy with the affidavit. For the newspaper to dispatch a reporter to Quebec just to prove that Mrs. Robinson was not one of the Wood sisters would have been a major story in itself.

It is unclear exactly where the *Whig* stood regarding the truthfulness of Wood's claim. The *Whig* went on to challenge those who were continuing the rumor to place their proof that Mrs. Robinson was a member of the Wood family "before the public". The *Whig* maintained that, if people continued the rumor without support, they must be "keeping up a delusion for sinister purposes." At the same time, they noted that, if Wood were not telling the truth, then he would be guilty of "unfilial and almost inhuman abandonment of a sister." The newspaper concluded this article with the remark that, if those behind the rumor did not come forward with proof, then they "should at least hold their peace."

On June 17, the question of the location of the meeting between Mr. Wood and the reporter was answered by yet another article in the *Whig*. Despite Wood's efforts, the rumors had not stopped. Never one to give up easily, Wood had submitted another article in which he said that he had come to Troy intent on meeting in person with Mrs. Robinson. When he arrived in Troy, he sent her a message that he had a series of ten questions that he would like to ask her. These questions, which would be easy for any of his sisters to answer, should be asked in front of her lawyer. Wood said that he had received a message that Henrietta agreed to meet with Pierson and him. He secured Pierson, and the two walked to the jail. By the time they reached the jail, Mrs. Robinson said that she would meet with Pierson or Wood, but not the two together. Wood went on to say that, as a result, he could not provide proof that the woman in jail was not his sister.

What Wood did not say in his affidavit was whether he or Pierson had met with Mrs. Robinson. According to Wilson's book, Wood did meet with her alone for one hour. Wood came out of that meeting and said that he had never seen the woman before.

While writing his book, Wilson met with Mrs. Robinson. She told a very different story about Wood's visit with her in the jail. Wilson summarized with an alteration of Lalla Rookh,

"She raised the veil – the man turned slowly around,

Looked at her – shrieked – and sunk upon the ground."

In Wood's final vindication, he explained his family's plight and supported Wilson's claim that he had actually met with Mrs. Robinson. "I know this woman never had relations with my family. I have striven assiduously, but unavailingly, to confront her in the presence of those whose previous knowledge of my family would enable them at once to determine the correctness of my statement." He added: "when the respectability and position of my family were thus assaulted, that common justice required that I should be afforded every facility to vindicate both." His statement makes it clear that Pierson must have had knowledge of the Wood family from the past; otherwise, why would Pierson have been chosen to accompany Wood to the jail to confront Mrs. Robinson. Wood could just as easily have chosen Beach, Townsend, Storer, or any of the other lawyers involved in the trial.

Assuming Wilson was correct when he stated that there was a meeting between Mrs. Robinson and Wood, it raises two questions. First, if it was Wood's goal to prove that Mrs. Robinson was not one of his sisters, why had he not given the list of questions to Pierson? The testimony at the trial established that it would have been easy to arrange for a jailer to stand by to overhear the answers. Second, assuming that Wood did meet with Mrs. Robinson, why would he have met for an hour in a jail with someone who was not his sister?

These letters were not the end of the issue. In an editorial in the *Times* of the next day, the question was raised as to why Mr. Willard was so insistent that Mrs. Robinson did not attend the Seminary. As the article indicates, the school can teach values, but that does not mean that every graduate will follow those same values throughout their lives. The *Times* also goes on to remind everyone that Mrs. Robinson never made the assertion that she was Emma Wood, but insisted on keeping her background a secret, even from her lawyers.

Like this author, the *Times* questioned how Mr. Willard could make a positive identification based solely on seeing only a hand and a forehead. The *Times* adds, "A hundred persons who had known Emma Wood saw Mrs. Robinson's forehead during the trial, and they did not come to the same conclusion that Mr. Willard did."

In effect, there was a belief among those who knew Emma as a student, and Mrs. Robinson, as a woman on trial for her life, that the two women could be the same person.

The question of Mrs. Robinson's identity was spreading, not just locally, but internationally. The *Montreal Transcript* published an article that, to many, finally resolved the issue. The article pointed out that Mrs. Robinson was the daughter of a lumber dealer in Quebec; she had married an officer in the First Royals. Her husband died a short time later, and she remarried, this time to a Dr. Robinson, whom she abandoned. The story in the *Transcript* so closely paralleled the rumors about Mrs. Robinson that many stopped the search at this point and accepted that this was her lineage.

The Troy newspapers were now pushed into a corner. They had contended that Mrs. Robinson was one of the Wood sisters; their sources were now being repudiated by the *Transcript's* article. Within a day, the Troy newspapers were able to put aside the *Transcript's* story by the discovery that there was indeed a woman described by the *Transcript*; however, there were two problems with the *Transcript's* findings. First, the woman written about in the *Transcript* married the second time to **Dr. Robertson,** not Robinson. Second, that the woman, Mrs. Robertson, died in the asylum in Hudson nine years earlier.

The answer to the issue continued to be the basis for numerous rumors over the course of the next several months. It was, however, most commonly believed that Mrs. Robinson was Emma Wood.

The Sentencing

Mrs. Robinson's trial ended in May, 1854, almost one year to the day from the funerals of Timothy Lanagan and Catherine Lubbee. As noted previously, Judge Harris had postponed her sentencing for what was called, at the time, a "temporary" period. As the summer leaves changed into the beautiful hues of fall, she waited. Eventually the leaves fell and snow provided the backdrop for the winter of 1854-55; still she waited. The dirty ash-covered snow melted, replaced by the dark greens of spring; all the while Mrs. Robinson remained in her cell in the Troy jail. While Mrs. Robinson sat in her cell, much transpired in the political community. One of the most important events, for Mrs. Robinson, was the election of a new governor.

Her lawyers had spent the year actively appealing for a new trial. In the meantime, she was still not sentenced. Making her wait was not logical, since, in the 1850's, the only sentence for murder in the first degree was death by hanging. For thirteen months, Mrs. Robinson resided in her cell. After her attack on Sheriff Price, she had only limited outbursts. It seems that she had finally accepted that she was convicted. Without having heard the actual words declaring her death, she appeared, during this period, more receptive to her eventual outcome.

Part of the change in her attitude may have been based on religion or, at the very least, probably had a spiritual foundation. If Henrietta Robinson was, in fact, one of the Wood sisters, then she had been raised in the Church of England. While in jail, she was visited by Father Peter Havermans, the Catholic priest from St. Mary's Church in Troy. Havermans and members of the Sisters of Charity had visited her almost daily. Through their ministrations, she

Rev. Peter Havermans

converted to Catholicism. Mrs. Robinson believed that she had accepted the forgiveness of Christ and was certain that she would be welcome in heaven.

***

In September of 1854, the grand jury that was seated at that time completed a tour of the jail. Members of this grand jury wanted to see the accommodations of Mrs. Robinson. This group was greeted very differently from the group who visited during the previous spring. Rather than hiding under her bed or making a mannequin, Mrs. Robinson was pleasant and received the men as guests in her accommodations. She did not disappoint the men; she wore her veil during their visit.

***

There was one visitor during the winter of 1854-55 who cast substantial light on the true identity of Mrs. Robinson. Wilson is the source of this story, which he undoubtedly learned from someone who worked in the jail. In true Wilson style, he does not disclose the name of her visitor, but refers to her simply as "Mary." The same name will be used in this work.

Perhaps she was feeling melancholy or perhaps just lonely, but during her second winter in jail, Mrs. Robinson asked the sheriff and his deputies if they would make inquiries into whether an Irish seamstress named "Mary" still lived in the area. When asked why, Mrs. Robinson said that she had known the woman when she was girl in Quebec. Mrs. Robinson went on to say that the woman subsequently moved to Troy. Hoping to learn more about the identity of Mrs. Robinson, the deputies made inquiries and found that there was a woman, who matched the description given by Mrs. Robinson, living in Schaghticoke (a town near Troy). A message was sent to "Mary" telling her that Mrs. Robinson would like to see her. Knowing she was being summoned by a woman who was trying to hide from everyone else, Mary made arrangements to get to Troy.

The reunion of the two women in the jail added considerable light to Mrs. Robinson's identity. There was no advance notice that "Mary" was going to arrive; when the woman was brought into the cell, she and Mrs. Robinson immediately recognized each other and hugged at length. Mrs. Robinson called the woman "Mary" and "Mary" said, during the embrace, "Charlotte, Charlotte is that you?" It was later learned that "Mary" had worked for a time as a seamstress in the home of a wealthy family in Quebec. She and one of the daughters, Charlotte, had developed a special bond. Later, when Charlotte left for Troy to attend the Seminary, "Mary" told the family that she was moving to Troy. The family asked that she deliver some personal items, including letters. "Mary" stopped by the Seminary to deliver the items. Realizing that she was in the area, the two women visited several times over the course of the two years Charlotte attended the Seminary. "Mary" had done some work for Charlotte, and the two had remained close. This is one of the only visits to Mrs. Robinson by someone who knew her as a girl.

Seeing the positive effect that "Mary" was having on Charlotte's temperament, the sheriff allowed her to stay. In fact, "Mary" moved into Mrs. Robinson's cell for one week, the two women sharing the same bed and the jail food. The two women conversed in ways that only old friends, reunited after a long absence, can understand. They reminded each other of the incidents that they shared. It was through this visit that the story of the doll and the story of the pond were both learned. It was during this one-week visit that Mrs. Robinson seemed to acknowledge that she was Charlotte Wood. Until now it had been universally believed that she was the other sister, Emma.

***

As the rumor that Mrs. Robinson was actually Charlotte Wood circulated, the wife of one of Beach's sons said that one way they could determine if it were Charlotte was by a crooked little finger. His wife had attended the Seminary at the same time as two of the Wood sisters, including Charlotte. She told the deputies that Charlotte had fallen from a horse when she was a girl and broken the little finger on her right hand; the finger had healed at an angle. The Charlotte Wood who attended the Seminary had developed a way of hiding the deformity by carrying a handkerchief in her hand. Mrs. Robinson had a crooked finger and did carry a handkerchief in her hand at all times.

There is also one other story that supports the position that Mrs. Robinson attended the Seminary. A minister dropped by the jail to visit Mrs. Robinson; when he got to her cell, he did not recognize the woman who stood before him. She recognized him, calling him by name. Mrs. Robinson told the minister how much she had enjoyed his services when she attended the Seminary.

***

It was not until May of 1855, that the upper courts in Albany heard arguments in the appeal requesting a second trial. Throughout the appeal process, Mrs. Robinson was represented by Job Pierson. Henry Hogeboom, the lawyer from Hudson, represented the People. There were two basic legal issues in the appeal. The first was exceptions made by the defense to the judge's charge to the jury; the second was a very technical issue involving notification before the trial began.

161

In his closing before the jury, Judge Harris had made two statements as to the use of alcohol and its effect on an insanity defense. The judge had even said, that "if the prisoner was intoxicated, even to the extent that she was unconscious of what she was doing, still the law holds her responsible for the act." The second statement was: "though the prisoner may have been excited by drink, at the time of the alleged offenses, even to such an extent as not to know what she was doing, she must answer for the consequences; her self-inflicted insanity must not be allowed to avail her for her defense. The law still imputes to her a murderous intent." The judge's statement was interpreted by the defense as referring to the intake of alcohol by free will. One of the defense's major points was that the intake of alcohol by Mrs. Robinson was the result of insanity, not the precursor.

The defense held that the judge's instructions were structured so that if the jurors believed that she was under the influence of alcohol, they should not find her insane. The defense believed that the instructions should have left open excessive use of alcohol, if the drinking itself was a result of insanity. What they had suggested was, "that if they (the jury) believed, from the evidence that the mind of the prisoner was, at the time of the alleged offense, in such a state that she could not distinguish between right and wrong, she was not responsible for her acts, and that they should find a verdict in her favor." This language left out the issue of involuntary drunkenness.

The defense's greatest hope lay in a ruling on the technical issue that the notification of the trial was improper. Both sides received an answer from the court – a refusal to hear the case any further. Because of the higher court's decision, it fell to the lower court to sentence Mrs. Henrietta Robinson.

Wilson was able to find a story that relates Mrs. Robinson's reaction to the news that she was about to be sentenced. On the ninth of June, she heard of the ruling by the higher court. She had the deputies gather candles; that night after the sun went down, she started to light the candles that she had collected. During this time candles were considered a luxury, especially during the long days of the summer when most people would light only one or two candles. With the outside work and long days of summer, most often people went to bed when it grew dark. As she started to light the candles, her room became brighter and brighter. To people passing by, it almost looked as though the jail were on fire. Mrs. Robinson could hear the sounds of people who had gathered to see the spectacle of light. She walked to the window; when her silhouette appeared in the window, there was a loud roar from those gathered below. Spontaneously, it became a game. The crowd would watch her window in anticipation of a glimpse of the "fallen woman"; in exchange, she would dance around her cell, intermittently passing before the window. On occasion she would stop and look down, the crowd would reward her with another loud roar. The entertainment ended as the candles slowly melted away, along with her dreams of a retrial.

In order to avoid a media and social frenzy, Judge Harris sought to sentence Mrs. Robinson as quietly as possible. On June 14, 1855, an unrelated trial ended; it happened that the same lawyers were involved in that case as in Mrs. Robinson's trial. Harris called on the lawyers to be present that afternoon so that he could pass sentence. Hearing the judge's request, Pierson asked that he be given time to talk to his client. He remembered all too well how she had acted when the verdict was handed down. Pierson wanted an opportunity to try to explain to Mrs. Robinson what was going to happen at the sentencing. Pierson had too much first-hand experience with Mrs. Robinson's handling stress, and he wanted to lessen the strain of the sentencing. Against his better judgment, Harris gave Pierson until the afternoon of June 19 to have his client prepared. Finally a date was set to end the trial of Mrs. Robinson; it had been more than two years since the crime and more than one year since the end of the trial.

During the intervening five days, the press and many citizens received word of the judge's intentions. At 3:10, on June 19, 1855, when Mrs. Robinson was brought before Harris, instead of the empty court room the judge wanted, he found himself facing a throng of people, including reporters from all of the regional newspapers. Each reporter gave a slightly different account of exactly what transpired in the court that afternoon. What follows here is the best compilation that could be made from the diverse stories.

Knowing what was about to transpire, Mrs. Robinson came

into the court dressed as finely as she had during her trial. As she had throughout her trial, her face was completely covered by a blue veil. On the arm of the sheriff, as if on a date, she walked into the chamber in a sprightly manner. Here, on this day, she would hear the words that would condemn her to the gallows. She walked up to her attorneys saying, in a voice loud enough for the reporters to hear clearly, "How do you do, Mr. Pierson?" There was a deliberate, polite, coolness in her address to Pierson. As she took her seat before the bar, Henrietta Robinson appeared to be totally composed.

Whether he dreaded the task, or not, will never be known; however, as if repeating a script used by countless of his predecessors, District Attorney Bingham rose and faced Judge Harris. His voice never wavered as he called out, "May it please the court, I have a motion to make in the matter of Henrietta Robinson." He took a breath before continuing, "She stands convicted of the murder of Timothy Lanagan." Looking in the direction of Mrs. Robinson, Bingham went on, "I am informed that the prisoner is now in the court room. If it please the court, I move the sentence of the law be now passed upon her." His remarks finished, he returned to the seat at the table, where he had sat all too often.

A hush had passed over the crowded court room. It is at moments like this, when we know the outcome, but not the reaction, that society takes on a sense of somber dignity. Everyone present that day realized that, in the next few moments, a period of Troy's history would come to its conclusion.

Pierson was always a gentleman; as such, he was composed as he remarked, "I have now nothing to say against the passing of the sentence in this case." At this point in the proceedings, there were some legal motions that were discussed, including amendments to some legal motions. The motions were technical, having no impact on the outcome of either the trial or the sentencing. Having won all of the legal motions he requested, Pierson went on to say the words being felt by all those present. He told the court that, "I have done all that I can, legally, for my client, to avert the sentencing that is about to take place. I have done all that is in my power to save the life of this poor woman. My exertions have been in vain" In reality, he felt that in addition to his legal efforts, he had also done all he could for her morally as well. Pierson went on, "I believe that my client has been unjustly condemned. Unfortunately, the Supreme Court has adjudicated otherwise and ordered that she must suffer death. This court is now in a position where it must pass sentence upon my client" (In New York, the Supreme Court at the time was the highest court in the state; in a reorganization a few years later, the Court of Appeals became the highest court and the Supreme Court became the lowest court.)

Pierson concluded his remarks, repeating some of the comments he had made previously; "I have nothing further to say against the passing of sentence. I have exhausted my power to save this poor woman. I consider that she should have a new trial, but the Supreme Court thought otherwise." It was at this point that Pierson showed his humanity, "I did all I could without hope of fee or reward of any kind, except the reward which the recollection of having diligently and faithfully sought to save a fellow-being, from what I consider an undeserved penalty, will afford." Perhaps Pierson's friendship with Mather had some other benefit than a fee or reward. He closed with a shot at the legal system. "I resign my unhappy client to her fate, and submit to the mandate that demands her sacrifice."

Judge Harris turned to Sheriff Price and ordered that all of those in attendance be seated. The spectators knew that the amount of time in court would be limited. Believing it better to hear than to be comfortable, those assembled had sacrificed a seat for the proximity of the front of the room. It took several minutes for the judge's decree, that all those assembled be seated, to be followed.

Eventually the confusion was overcome, and it was now up to the judge to say the words prescribed in the law. Harris turned to the prisoner and said, "Mrs. Robinson, have you any objections to removing the veil?"

Mrs. Robinson had been talking quietly to Pierson. When the request of the judge finally registered in her mind, she amazed those who had gathered in this hot court room. In front of this throng, Mrs. Robinson stood defiant. She threw her blue veil, the source of her nickname, the Veiled Murderess, over her bonnet. After sitting through hearings and a trial with the veil on, no one had expected to actually witness her remove the covering. For the first time since her arrest, people could see her face. Despite the restrictions of her confinement and the stress of the trial, she was considered to be attractive. Perhaps she was not quite beautiful, but Henrietta Robinson showed that she had the refinement and presence to stand out in a crowd. Now the question of her age was narrowed. Seeing her face for the first time, it was believed that she was in her late twenties, perhaps even thirty.

Seeing the effect that her exposed face was having on the crowd, Henrietta Robinson was heard to laugh. Once more, she had shown that she was in control. If she could not have power over the outcome, she would at least manipulate the steps in the process.

Judge Harris spoke in a loud clear voice. "It is my painful duty, Mrs. Robinson, to inform you that the Supreme Court at Albany has denied the application of your counsel for a new trial in your case, and has ordered this court to proceed to pass the sentence required under the law upon you. Have you anything to say before that sentence is passed?"

If Henrietta Robinson was anything, she was emotionally strong when she needed to be. "Yes, I have much to say, but I know I will be interrupted." Her words were an attack on the judicial system as she had experienced it.

Assuming that her words meant that she would not make a statement, Judge Harris continued, "You have been convicted of the willful murder of Timothy Lanagan."

Judge Harris had misread Mrs. Robinson; she was not finished speaking. "Yes, but it was upon false evidence." She then turned her sharp tongue on the judge; "You have all conspired against me! Shame, judge; I have been persecuted because of John C. Mather. Shame!" Perhaps shouting rather than speaking would be a better description of her presentation.

The judge, who was used to controlling situations in his court, carried on, explaining his rationalization for what he was about to say. "The law has proceeded with a slow but steady step toward judgment. You have proceeded through its every phase until you have arrived at this condition." If he had stopped there, in all probability, Mrs. Robinson would have remained calm. Unfortunately, he felt compelled to continue, expressing in no uncertain terms the values of the Victorian era. "You have lost all. To you, life is lost," a long, steady, thoughtful pause held the courtroom's full attention, "character is gone," another long pause and then, "friends are gone."

Mrs. Robinson looked him directly in the eye and said in a cold strong voice, "No, no, not all."

Although he had proven that he could postpone a decision for a prolonged period, Harris was not one to dawdle when he finally accepted that an unpleasant task needed to be addressed. He tried again to lecture the prisoner. "If I thought you would listen to me," again he paused, this time for effect, "But I know you would not."; yet another pause followed, " I would advise you to abandon this fruitless struggle with the world." Indicating what he thought of her erratic behavior, the judge went on, "I would advise you to throw off this feigned insanity, and prepare to meet, with true womanly resignation, the fate that awaits you." The judge exhibited his moral indignation one more time, saying, "Life to you is not worth possessing. Your honor and virtue are gone." These words show the true underlying values that Mrs. Robinson had fought against, both in society and within herself. In Victorian times, you were either virtuous, or you were not; there was no gray, only total black or pure white. To the judge, as to so many of his peers, once a woman slipped off the paved road of life, she could not get back into the lane. Worse yet, an indiscretion in one area was a misdeed in every area of life.

Judge Harris also had indicated what he felt about her insanity; he had called it "feigned." After all he had seen, after all he had heard about, could he have harbored a sense that she was only faking the insanity? Had that sense been passed on to the jury? Did Harris really believe that a sane person could have killed two persons without the slightest motive?

Mrs. Robinson, as a lady, was, in some ways, one of the best examples of a woman raised under the rules of her time. She had shown throughout the trial, and in her life before the murders, that she had culture and manners. At the same time, by leaving her husband and children in England, she demonstrated that she was a woman who stood against those same rules. She dismissed the judge, "Don't trouble yourself about that, if you please, judge."

In another account of the same event Mrs. Robinson was reported to have spelled out her answer to the judge, "P-o-o-h!"

Knowing he had met his emotional match, Judge Harris continued his effort to address her values – or at least his. "I am aware that you would listen to nothing from me. I shall, therefore, without further remark, proceed to pass sentence upon you."

With a strong, righteous, voice, Harris persisted. "The sentence of the court is that you, Henrietta Robinson, be detained in the County Prison until the third day of August next, and that on that day between the hours of 10 o'clock in the forenoon and 2 in the afternoon, you will be hanged by the neck until you be dead, and may God in his infinite mercy save your soul."

In her most intimidating voice, Henrietta Robinson responded to the judge's words, "You had better pray for your own soul, sir." Mrs. Robinson then wanted to continue to address the court. Those in the room could sense that the drama happening before them was not over. The audience sat in silence, awaiting the next act. Knowing nothing could be gained by any words she wanted to express at this point, Pierson rose and tried to get her to remain silent. "Why should I remain quiet!" Her words echoed throughout the packed room. "What for? I am the victim of a political conspiracy, which has been calculated to crush an innocent man. All have deserted me. Martin I. Townsend has deserted me. Sheriff Price is a shameless, heartless, bastard."

Pierson had heard enough. He called to her, "Be quiet!".

She was not quiet, but instead directed her words directly to Pierson. Her tone was measured and, for the first time that day, her words could not be discerned throughout the room. In the heat of the moment, one name could be heard; Mrs. Robinson said, in a volume that was clear, the name of John C. Mather. At the very sound of his name, those in attendance erupted in verbal pandemonium. The court room, which had been silent, awaiting every word, had heard the one name that they wanted to be confirmed from her lips. They now had heard the woman, who had been silent throughout the trial, articulate the name of John C. Mather. The connection was true! She had been the mistress of one of the most powerful men in the State.

Judge Harris tried to restore order. "It is particularly desirable that the audience should remain seated." The sound of his gavel and the tone of his voice finally prevailed in quieting, if not silencing, the assemblage. "It is hoped that no one will follow the prisoner to the carriage. The sheriff will remove Mrs. Robinson from the room."

Price, a strong, effective man, knew that Mrs. Robinson was capable of many different and unpredictable reactions. Despite having experienced Mrs. Robinson's aspersions cast upon his name only minutes before, he knew that, in dealing with her, a calm approach was best. He leaned over and asked her to accompany him out of the room. She turned and looked directly at her jailer. Her eyes had that menacing quality that Price dreaded. The situation could have gone either way, calm or loud. The response was to be decided by Mrs. Robinson, and by no one else. Her eyes had taken on a glint as she pulled the veil back over her face.

Although she rarely spoke during her trial, Mrs. Robinson would have the last word on this day. She pointed her finger directly at the judge and said, "May the Judge of Judges be your Judge!" Ironically, this appears to be the beginning of the curse. It would be a few years before the curse would begin to manifest itself, but once it started it would effect so many lives.

The veil back in place, her face was again protected from the scrutiny of the people. Mrs. Robinson walked down the aisle and left the court room. She was followed to the carriage by most of those who had gathered. The crowd had ignored the judge's request just as Mrs. Robinson had done only moments before.

***

It was now time for Mrs. Robinson to prepare for her own death. She began by giving away personal items to the people who, she believed, had supported her during the long ordeal. Among her possessions were: two gold chains, twelve twenty-dollar gold pieces, one silver cake basket, eight silver forks, three black silk dresses, one plaid silk dress, one embroidered silk dress, three satin dresses, one green rule silk, one linen traveling dress, one velvet dress, three morning wrappers, two velvet cloaks, three shawls, twenty four handkerchiefs, undergarments, gloves and hats.

The Women's Issue

"Condemned by a tribunal of men to suffer the penalty of laws which she can break but not make." Thus ended a story about

169

the conditions under which Mrs. Robinson had lived; the article appeared in Horace Greeley's newspaper, the *New York Tribune*. This article appeared in July, 1855, approximately six weeks after the sentencing of Mrs. Robinson by Judge Harris.

As if this story did not have enough twists, the sentencing of Mrs. Robinson to death by hanging made her plight the cause for two social movements. The 1850's saw the beginning of an organized women's movement. One of the first women to take a leadership role in revising social issues was a woman named Mrs. E. Oakes Smith, who wrote a thesis on the plight of women entitled *"Woman and Her Needs"*. Mrs. Smith had become known in large part because of her thesis which appeared as a series of articles in Greeley's *Tribune*.

The 1850's was also the beginning of a movement to end capital punishment as a recourse in a civilized society. In the case of Mrs. Robinson, the two groups, those opposed to capital punishment and those opposed to a male dominated legal structure could join together. Both groups organized and movements to have her sentence commuted were undertaken by diverse groups.

Although there were earlier rumblings about universal suffrage, the movement in many ways expanded only when women started to take their stands on political and social issues. The plight of Mrs. Robinson, as she awaited her hanging, was one of the best examples available of a woman's tribulations. The chronicle of the life of Henrietta Robinson fell right into Mrs. Smith's social activist agenda. Among Mrs. Smith's issues was the sentencing of women to death by hanging. She was also consumed by the effects of insanity on a person's sentence. Mrs. Smith believed firmly in: the rights of women to, enter the professions, in this case, specifically, to be lawyers the rights of women to be tried by a jury of their peers, which she interpreted as a jury comprised of at least 50% women, the rights of women to vote, and, most importantly, the rights of women to serve as legislators.

It was not that Mrs. Smith believed Mrs. Robinson to be innocent of the charges against her. Mrs. Smith was a social activist; to her, the issue was the inability of a woman to receive justice in a man's world. In the second paragraph of her story in the *Tribune*, Mrs. Smith says, "I presume there is no doubt of her guiltiness." Mrs. Smith challenged society to move from the brutality of barbarism to an enlightened and socially responsible new order. To get her message across, Mrs. Smith wrote a series of letters and visited Mrs. Robinson in the jail.

The *New York Times* also took up the cause of commuting the sentence of Mrs. Robinson; their position was, "Her weakness is her defense." The *New York Times* reported in late July, that they were becoming more certain every day that capital punishment was a misconceived idea, but that they were already certain it was a bad idea in the case of women. Unlike Mrs. Smith, the *New York Times* felt that her conviction was "not entirely free of doubt." The newspaper also questioned the issue of her sanity. The *New York Times,* in calling on Governor Clark to commute the sentence, said that to proceed with this execution "would inspire the public mind with horror and disgust."

The Troy Daily Whig built its argument, regarding the commuting of the sentence, on a story that appeared in the *New York Express*. The *Express* held that Mrs. Robinson should be hanged. The newspaper reasoned that to commute her sentence was to give women a free hand to become assassins; that, by freeing her of the burden of the death penalty, society was freeing all women from just laws. They said that, if women could not suffer the penalty of death, why should they have to suffer the penalty of prison. The *Express* extended the argument to the point of absurdity. The *Whig* in contrast, held that the reasoning of the *Express* regarding punishment of women was correct, but that it did not apply to Mrs. Robinson's case. The *Whig* reasoned that her sentence should be commuted because they questioned the finding of the jury. They harbored reasonable doubt about her guilt and could only reason that, if she were guilty, it was because she was insane. The *Whig* went so far as to characterize the doubt as, "not a fanciful but a substantial one." Assuming the *Whig* was right in questioning her guilt, that would leave Mrs. Lanagan as the perpetrator.

Even in the direst of situations, there is often someone who can find a reason to laugh. In late June, there was a rumor circulating that Mrs. Robinson had been assured that Governor Clark would commute her sentence, even before it was pronounced. The rumor was that, because of this assurance, she acted so outrageously at her sentencing. The *Albany Atlas* attacked the Governor, who was opposed to the consumption of alcohol; they said that the Governor would pardon the arsenic, but not the beer.

Mrs. Smith did not stop at merely writing about the predicament of Mrs. Robinson. She took it upon herself to come to Troy and visit with the lady who had become her "cause". On Saturday July 28, the *Tribune* carried the following story, which was carried on the following Monday in the *Whig*. The story, because it comes from a person who actually talked with Mrs. Robinson while she was awaiting her death, is worthy of printing in its entirety. The article shows how this socially liberal person envisioned the behavior of those "out of the norm".

"I did not, when I went to Troy for the purpose of visiting the unhappy woman (Mrs. Robinson) in her gloomy cell, design to make any public expression of what I saw or heard, but her case is one so peculiar, and she is evidently of an insane organization – so evidently, from the first, cursed with a disjointed and irresponsible mental and moral sense, that it seems desirable to analyze her case somewhat. Further than this, she has most unquestionably been "more sinned against that sinning." No hand has been extended to aid and protect her in her weakness, while many have aided in her downward tendency, and with such the guilt must rest.

I doubt much if she could have well been held to the decorums of life. Phrenologically, her brain is low above the ears, and her course black hair grows down upon the forehead even lower than that upon the bust of the celebrated antique of Clite. She has two projections in the region of what is called Constructiveness, extending backward, which of themselves would be sufficient to throw the whole character out of balance. When you add to this brain a refined, lady-like form, rounded and compact, with the temperament of the highest and most excitable kind, it will easily be seen that education might retard and modify her destiny, but would hardly serve to recreate her into a reliable or very safe character.

She evidently is possessed of a remarkable healthy organization, capable of great endurance, and indicating longevity. Her eyes have a look of force and vitality, and when not excited by an insane mood, are really fine. She is perhaps thirty, and though an idealist would never call her beautiful, she is quite perfect in kind, and a vulgar mind would call her handsome.

She talks fluently with a ready use of language and appropriate imagery. As I sat by her, gathering up my feet from the floor, for the mice were having a perfect carnival about the neatly kept room, I could not bring my mind to think that this young creature, full of health, with nerves so delicately strung, would in less than ten days, lie an inanimate clod, and that, too, by the hands of violence. She had talked with men so candidly, often with such a childlike simplicity, laughing even over some bygone experience, and then weeping like a poor, ill-treated child, that I ventured to say as much to her.

"Yes," she replied, "a week from next Friday my soul will be with God; I want to die; I am sick of this cold, wicked world, where I cannot trust anybody. Oh! How I long to go home to God."

I could not look harshly and coldly upon the poor weeping Magdalen. I took her little pale hand in mine and wept with her. As yet she had talked perfectly sane. She seemed like a very excitable woman, but not in the least like an insane one.

One thing was noticeable in my interview. She was reclining upon the bed, and sat also upon the side of it. Her plain white dress, or robe rather, was fastened at throat and wrist, thus concealing her whole person, while a large dark blue veil was thrown over her head hiding her face partially. When her mood was gentle or religious, whenever her own consciousness was in the ascendant, her fingers moved uneasily about her neck. She would pull the collar away from her throat and swallow. This was very touching.

'But I have come to see you and to help save you from the final penalty, and in that case you would be willing to live.'

"No, no; I want to go home to my God; I am prepared

173

for death now. The mode is nothing to me now that I am at peace with God; He is more merciful than men. He will forgive me and allow my death to atone for my evil life. No, I want to die, and I long for the day to come. My dress is all ready – very decent it is. I shall be carried out [her fingers were touching the side of her neck] and die. No one will see my face. I shall be very still, and my Savior [lifting her eyes] will pity me. The Sisters promise me that I shall not be seen. They will bury me away where I shall not be taken up. They have promised to stay with me and to receive my body and all this is better than to live and perhaps lead an evil life again, and then die unprepared and forsaken of God. Oh no, dear, do not try to save me."

Surely the weakest heart – the wickedest heart that ever beat in a woman's bosom – has a spot over which an angel might rejoice; a dim and solitary chamber, which might be swept and garnished, and made an altar-place for the good Father.

'But if you go to prison or a hospital and preserve this frame of mind, you can do good to others; you can teach the ignorant and comfort the suffering, and take care of the sick or dying.'

"I don't know, I don't know, it is better for me to die; I might live thirty years in a prison; death seems better."

I looked at the lithe, active make, and could easily divine that imprisonment would be the greater penalty. I then told her the melancholy story of Margaret Divine, whom I believe to be entirely innocent of the crime for which she is convicted to twenty years of solitary imprisonment in the Newark, New Jersey Penitentiary. A child of fifteen, losing the best years of her life in a prison while hardened ruffianly villains are pardoned out. This girl, so young, so gentle, so hopeless, wearying out her life in the prison of a foreign land, affects me greatly; and Mrs. Robinson listened and wept; and shuddered at the recital.

"What a pity," she exclaimed, "they did not convict her."

'The public would not allow of the question.'

"But they will let me die?"

174

I shook my head.

"They will, they must. Oh, I am so sick of the world. Look here, please, my poor husband and children do not know where I am. They know nothing of all this. My father and mother are both dead; I have concealed my family name; while I live people are curious to know about me – when I am dead all will die with me. I have promised my brother to be very still; to die without betraying anything, and when I am gone I shall cease to worry and distress my family. Here I am shut out from the world, of no use in it, sick of it. Oh, let me go home to my God."

There was a manly courage and good sense in this forlorn desire for death. It shows, also that the fear of it may be overcome in many ways.

'If you are executed, you will be the last woman who will endure the penalty in our country. It will raise a storm of indignant protest, which will compel our rulers to annul the statute, at least where a woman is to be the victim.'

She smiled in a very sweet and heavenly manner: "Then there shall be some good in my death. Is not God very good if he will permit a sinful creature like me, not only to atone for my wicked life by this violent death, but may even allow some good to grow out of it."

'You are a Catholic?'

"I am now. And since I have had some one to talk to me, to tell me truly about myself, and my duty to God, I am a great deal happier. The Sisters of Charity come and talk to me very kindly; they tell me not to wish to live, but to take God's mode of drawing me back to himself, patiently and willingly."

This was very sweet and gave even an elevated expression to her handsome but unspirited face.

'Are you willing to remove your veil?'

"Oh yes, for you, but I do not like to have strangers come and stare at me. On my trial I felt I could not; I could not be looked at. It seemed to me I should make other women ashamed."

She then laid aside her veil and showed me her hair

beginning to fall off, and her head much too large for the vital region except the lungs. -She smiled like a child when I pressed her temples, and expressed my sympathy for the grief she must have endured, and the trial which would disturb and madden such an organization. Here she wept.

'Will you tell me truly whether you are guilty of the crime for which you are condemned? What you may say will not harm you in the least.'

Her eyes assumed a wild expression.

"No, I am not guilty. These people were good to me; sometimes when others were unkind, they were good to me. The came to me when I was sick, and sent their children to stay with me. I never treated a human being ungratefully. My heart is a kind one. I have with my own hands taken care of rich people and cooked up things for the poor, and have helped them as much as I could. Now these enemies who accuse me know that I am not guilty – that I never dreamed of poisoning my friends. I don't know about it; [she began to talk wildly] I had been sick; I was mad for a while because _____ gave me something that took away my senses. I try to think over a great many things that happened, and I can't understand them. I can't tell exactly how I got here. I know I am a wicked woman, but I did not do that. I am the victim of a conspiracy. A political party wished to crush John C. Mather and Myron H. Clark and so they took me up. They could do it, you know– I, a poor woman."

'You have confessed everything to our priest?'

" Oh, yes. He knows I am innocent; but he tells me it is better for me to die, and so I will die."

'Were you happily married? Are you willing to let me know all about your early life?'

"Oh, yes. I was married very young and to a man I could not love. He was a good man, but I did not love him, and my first sin was in deserting my family." Much that she here told me of her parentage and family and her sorrowful, often tragic experiences, is not essential to this communication. I am convinced she has no consecutive memory of the past. She thinks she talked coherently, when much of what she says is mere jargon. The mood of mind is entirely distinct from her religious one, the latter being a new one and a very harmonious one in her present exigency, enabling her to ignore the past and look calmly into the brief space of life before her revealing a never-ending, blissful future. It seems as if she had arisen from a terrible chaos, and she dreads life lest she should again relapse into it.

Turbulent as has been her career with her stormy passions, she could not recall it without a shudder; and yet she laughed wildly and gesticulated in almost frantic manner more than once. As it regards the past, her whole mind is in fragments. She remembers indeed 'a mass of things, but naught distinctively."

Before I left the prisoner she gave me a message for the Governor, begging me to deliver it to him faithfully, which of course I did not fail to do: "Tell him there is a political party wishing to put him out of office. They wish to crush Myron H. Clark and John C. Mather; and if he commutes my sentence they will make political capital out of it; and I would rather die than be used as an instrument to ruin a good man. Tell him to let me die as I wish."

Mrs. Smith provided us with the only in-depth examination of Mrs. Robinson. It is interesting that, although Mrs. Robinson had made a religious conversion she still held that she was innocent of the crime that she had been convicted of committing. Was her denial because she was not guilty, or was she just unable to face the seriousness of her act?

***

Under pressure from many factions, including petitions signed by judges, prosecutors and other notables, on Friday, July 27, Governor Clark commuted Mrs. Robinson's sentence. Under the terms of his order, she was to spend the rest of her life in prison.

Hearing of the Governor's decision on Friday afternoon, Sheriff Price was ready to be rid of his notorious prisoner; however, he could not act until he had the official order from the governor. Mrs. Robinson also learned of the governor's decision on Saturday morning, but, unlike Price, she could begin to act immediately. As has been noted, in jail she was allowed to have her own possessions. In prison, she would not be allowed the same luxury. Even though it was the hot days of July, Mrs. Robinson started a fire in the woodstove of her cell. In what would be depicted as her last tantrum in the jail, Mrs. Robinson burned most of her possessions. Her furniture became ashes. Over the course of the time between her sentencing and the commuting of the sentence, she had given away most of her clothes and rugs.

The *Whig* talked about her desire not to have her sentence commuted. They interviewed Price, who said that she opposed the efforts of her "pretended friends." According to Price, these were the same individuals who had made up the stories about her insanity. Price said that she did not want to live, but wanted to have the whole matter over. She wanted to be "spared the tortures of living longer."

On Saturday afternoon, wearing all of the possessions she still owned, the rest having been given away, Mrs. Robinson, in the company of Sheriff Price, boarded the 4:00 p.m. train bound for Sing Sing Prison. The news of the commuting of her sentence created speculation that she would be moved to a prison. Despite Sheriff Price's best efforts to keep her departure a secret, many people knew the train schedule and lined the streets waiting for a chance to see the Veiled Murderess one last time. Again the crowd was to be disappointed since she was closely veiled, so they only witnessed a silhouette. As she walked through the train station, she was recognized by many of the others who were present.

Sheriff Price was the only person to accompany her on the trip to prison. He told Wilson of her mood swings along this ominous trip. At times she seemed not to understand where she was going, talking instead about returning to her home in Quebec. At other times she seemed totally cognizant of her plight and broke down and cried. At one point she asked Price to intercede and make arrangements for her to be able to wear her own clothes rather than the garb required in prisons. In Poughkeepsie, she had a light meal, which she ate with perfect lady-like decorum. Her emotions ran out before she reached the prison, and she was tired, almost listless.

Perhaps because the hour was late, the prison was not expecting them. The guard was not present, but there was a group of young people gathered in the prison's entry. Sheriff Price announced Mrs. Robinson much the way people were introduced at a ball or dinner party at the time. The young people seemed to be taken completely off guard by the presence of such a renowned criminal. They remained silent, as if a collective awe had passed over the group. Mrs. Robinson turned to Price and said, "What queer people they are; they have no manners." She then called upon Price to take her home; she had no desire to stay in a place where the people had no manners. When Price didn't answer, she urged him to call for her brother "William" to come and get her.

When the officer came to admit her, he asked the routine questions: name, age, place of birth. Mrs. Robinson just laughed, turning to the sheriff and saying, "Why, this man is crazy!" The guard did not find her behavior amusing and yelled at her, demanding answers. His agitated behavior only made her laugh even louder.

The guard again asked her age. She responded that to ask was "impertinent." The only question that she answered was with respect to her place of birth. She told the guard that she was from Quebec. When the guard threatened her with punishment if she did not answer his questions correctly, she laughed again. Finally, and perhaps because the sheriff was there as a witness, the guard said that he would finish the admission in the morning, and either she would give him answers or "she would get cold water." She turned to the sheriff, laughing, and said, "That fellow is surely crazy."

They inspected the small package that she had brought with her. There, in addition to the usual things a prison traveler might take, was a rope five feet long.

Who Was Mrs. Robinson
Part III

In the 1870's, because of a class reunion at the Seminary, there was a renewed interest in the identity of Mrs. Robinson. *The Troy Times* carried an article, some time later, that they believed to demonstrate proof that Mrs. Robinson was not one of the Wood sisters. It was said that William Wood escorted his sister, Charlotte Elliott, to the reunion. The Wood family had not notified the school in advance, so there were no reporters actually at the reunion. There were several women present who, when interviewed later, said that the woman in attendance was Charlotte.

At the time of the article, the *Troy Times* had been in contact with a former official from Sing Sing Prison. According to the official, Mrs. Robinson had a very different identity from that of one of the Wood sisters. The newspaper claimed that the woman known as Mrs. Robinson was English by birth. She came to know of the Wood sisters through an "acquaintance of theirs in England." When the woman who was now in prison was convicted of infanticide in England, she was sentenced to Van Dieman's Land. Some of the woman's influential friends had the sentence commuted to banishment. On the ship that she boarded when she left England bound for America, she was befriended by a well-respected woman from New York City. The woman offered her employment and a place to stay. According to this unnamed official, the woman, who would come to be known as Mrs. Robinson, left her benefactor's home after a few weeks and headed for Boston. In Boston, she, "got into bad company and pursued a life of wanton." Despite her lifestyle in Boston, the lady whom she had befriended received occasional correspondence. Supposedly, the husband of the woman from New York was with Governor Clark when he met with Mrs. Robinson in Sing Sing. At that meeting, the husband showed Mrs. Robinson the letters that had been mailed to his wife. In front of the Governor, Mrs. Robinson admitted to duplicity in posing as one of the Wood sisters.

A very different narrative about the reunion appeared in the New York City newspapers. These newspapers said that the Wood family realized that the reunion would provide the perfect opportunity to stop the belief that Mrs. Robinson was Charlotte Wood, thus removing the yoke of disgrace from the family name. The Wood family exerted some considerable influence to pull off a simple scheme. They had Charlotte brought back to Troy from Sing Sing. While she was in Troy, she was housed in the jail. On the night of the reunion, she was dressed in "resplendent attire." She took the arm of her brother, who had her name called out as "Mrs. Elliott". The next day she was spirited back to Sing Sing.

The Press tried, at least a little, to get to the truth. They claimed to interview one of the lawyers who was involved in the trial, a man who had visited Mrs. Robinson in prison. Although the Press did not name the lawyer, the only one to fit that description, who was still alive, was Martin Townsend. His comment, regarding the establishment of the identity of Henrietta Robinson, was that it was "a romance from start to finish." Townsend went on to say that Mrs. Robinson was neither beautiful nor intelligent. He used, as a proof, one incident in which she said, "and then they leaved." It was Townsend's belief that the woman was of French birth, and "the woman never attended the Willard Seminary." Townsend, who knew William Wood, acknowledged that there was a strong resemblance between the two. It was Townsend's belief that Mrs. Robinson was William Wood's illegitimate daughter.

Curse

"The sins of the fathers shall be visited on the sons."

At several points during the trial, Henry Hogeboom intimated that Mrs. Robinson had the ability to place men under her spell. In Hogeboom's mind, her powers made men want to be near her and to fulfill her needs. To Hogeboom, these forces explained why so many men visited her in jail. Hogeboom believed these alleged "spells" fell upon men regardless of their station in life. From the most humble of butchers, who would tie her garter in a public market, to the most esteemed lawyers in the region, who brought her snuff, Hogeboom reasoned that, around Mrs. Robinson, men lost control of their sense of right and wrong. Hogeboom believed that she ignited some indefinable desires, which then were fueled by the necessity to satisfy her desires. He was so concerned about her abilities that, in his closing arguments, he even called upon the members of the jury to do their duty and not to fall victim to those same charms.

A series of events occurred in the lives of those involved in the trial of Mrs. Robinson that imply that she could cast both spells and curses. The words "curse" and "spell" are often used as synonyms; both words are used to express the idea that some external force can or has been placed upon something or someone. A spell, however, can be either positive or negative, while a curse is considered to be only negative.

If Mrs. Robinson could cast a spell, if she knew that she had the power, it may provide a very different explanation for her wearing the veil during the trial. Perhaps she did not want to cast some magic over too many.

If we assume that Hogeboom's theory is true, it would explain why at least two men's behavior regarding her was personally unwise. It is apparent that John C. Mather was so enamored of her that when she left him, he pursued her to Boston, even though the exposure of their relationship would endanger his political career. Even after she leveled Sheriff Price with a candlestick, he remained one of the leading proponents of commuting her sentence.

One could easily question Hogeboom's premise that she could cast spells of attraction, but it would appear from the evidence that Mrs. Robinson could cast curses and blessings. Those curses were placed on those who did not act in her best interests at the trial, while those who supported her lived long and respected lives. Any controls she had over the lives of the people of Troy did not appear to end when she went to prison. In examining the lives of the families of the men involved in the trial, one has to wonder if, in addition to any spells she may have been able to work, Mrs. Robinson had the ability to curse those who had failed her? At the same time, did she guard those who had supported her until the end?

The Players

From all the records, it appears that District Attorney Bingham understood from the beginning that the case was beyond his capacity. To offset the heavy hitters of Beach, Pierson and Townsend, Bingham hired Van Santvoord and the out-of-towner, Hogeboom. The actual prosecution of the case against Mrs. Robinson was conducted almost exclusively by Henry Hogeboom and George Van Santvoord. Anson Bingham played a minimal, almost insignificant, role in the trial. During the trial, the only witness who really testified against Mrs. Robinson was Anna Lanagan. The only other person who seemed to have a serious problem with Mrs. Robinson was Sheriff Price, and his behavior wavered between positive and negative.

Mrs. Robinson's defense involved primarily the attorneys William Beach, Martin Townsend, and Job Pierson. Like Bingham, attorneys Storer and Smith took minor roles, saying virtually nothing during the trial. The only defense witness who cast aspersions against Mrs. Robinson was the lawyer-witness Richard C. Jennyss. Pierson's support and opinions were measurably different from those of his co-defenders in that he believed that there never should have been a defense offered. Pierson believed that the prosecution had failed to prove its case, so he didn't want to put forward the insanity argument.

The last major player in the trial was Judge Ira Harris. During the trial, he was considered to be generally fair, but his closing charge to the jury was biased and condemning.

The last player was from Mrs. Robinson's personal life. As

185

was seen in Mrs. Smith's letter, she supported John C. Mather until the end.

The Blessing

One might wonder what happened to the three men who took Mrs. Robinson's side, the men who sincerely tried to help her. If one were to believe in a curse, then is it not unreasonable to believe equally in a blessing. If that is the case, then Pierson, Bontecou and Hegemen deserved to be blessed.

Job Pierson was the defense attorney who did not even want to put on a defense. He was the man who stood by Mrs. Robinson throughout the trial. He led the fight for her appeal and stood beside her when she heard the death sentence being imposed by Judge Harris. Pierson was the attorney who reduced the arguments to their simplest form. He had presented to the jury a summation that would have inevitably resulted in either a hung jury or an acquittal, if not for the charge given by Judge Harris. Job died a natural death in April of 1860. His obituary was indeed impressive and showed the support and respect he had enjoyed throughout his life.

During the trial, **Dr. Reed Bontecou** was placed on the stand as a witness for the prosecution. By the time Beach finished the cross-examination, Bontecou became one of Mrs. Robinson's best witnesses. Bontecou was the coroner who examined Mrs. Robinson on the night she was arrested and who led the search of her home. He was questioned regarding Mrs. Robinson's possessions and her sanity.

Bontecou was a colonel with the Union forces during the Civil War, having several assignment, including head surgeon on a hospital ship involved in the blockade of Charleston. He was considered to be a brilliant surgeon, and his methods were copied for years. During his life, he was the author of articles in several major medical journals.

Dr. Bontecou outlived Mrs. Robinson. He was 83 at the time of his death in 1907. An example of his good fortune lies in the fact that he was only sick for one week. He collapsed while climbing the stairs in one of his patient's homes. He enjoyed excellent health and practiced medicine, with his only son, until one week before he died.

Dr. Reed Bontecou   **Dr. Hegeman**

The versatile **William Hegemen** was not satisfied to be simply the doctor/jailor. After the trial, he went to Albany Law School and passed the bar, although he never practiced. Hegemen became a professional baseball player and a judge of horse racing; he was an auctioneer, justice of the peace and coroner. Hegemen married in 1860; he fathered three sons and two daughters. One of his daughters adopted the stage name of Beatrice Cameron and became a well-known actress.

Dr. William Hegemen was 80 years old when he died in 1908.; he was survived by his wife and all of his children. Not only was he a good friend, he was a successful businessman.

The Curse

George Van Santvoord was a local intellectual legend. He was the son of a minister, from one of the Old Dutch families whose parish was in rural Schodack. He attended Union College then studied law in Kinderhook. After marrying into the wealthy Van Schaick family, he and his young wife moved to Indiana where he wrote and published a book on Indiana justice. A few years later, he returned to a farm in Schodack and became a rail commuter to his law office in Troy.

Before the trial began, in addition to a series of articles, he published his second book, which was a collection of the biographies of several Chief Justices of the Supreme Court. He would go on to write several other books in diverse genre, but most in the areas of law or history. In the election following the trial, Van Santvoord replaced Bingham as the county's district attorney.

In April, 1863, forty-three year old Van Santvoord was waiting for a train at the South Albany Depot. He was not looking as a second train backed into the yard. Van Santvoord was struck by the train, and the wheels rolled over his right arm. His writing arm was severed; he lost blood rapidly. Those who were nearby carried him into the station and sent for a physician. He died twenty minutes later.

The man who was most proud of his writing, watched as he lost his writing hand. The man who had crushed Mrs. Robinson's insanity defense by his claims that she was intoxicated had himself been crushed.

William A. Beach had an American heritage that rivaled those of the early presidents. He was born into a family of lawyers; he had a great uncle who was on the Supreme Court of the United States. Beach was raised to be a lawyer, and he raised his sons to be lawyers. Beach had four sons: Miles, John, William A. Beach Jr., and Warren. Warren was named for his great-uncle who was a judge in New York. Miles Beach was named after his grandfather, a wealthy merchant and the second postmaster of Saratoga Springs. By the time he was in his late twenties, Miles was a partner in his father's office.

Miles went on to be the mayor of Troy, serving from 1870-72. Twenty years later, Miles was a Justice of the State Supreme Court. In the 1890's, because of wild speculations and the stock market crash of 1893, he lost, literally, everything. One of the stockbrokers, whom Miles did not pay, sued for his loss. Miles could not repay the debt, and the broker knew it. The broker had to settle for embarrassment of Miles by making him acknowledge on the stand that he had a mistress, by whom he had two children, living in New Jersey. Miles retained his position as a judge but lost his father's fortune, and he lost his wife. He died at his suite in the Waldorf Astoria with only his brother, Warren, at his side. But it was Beach's third son, who showed the greatest promise, and who paid for his father's pride.

Named after his father, the younger W. A. Beach was considered to have the greatest potential for carrying on the family legal tradition. He was intelligent, handsome, and a champion debater. William Jr. was so academically talented that he entered Williams College as a sophomore, skipping his freshman year. In college, he was a member of the Literary Society and played on the baseball team. When he finished college in 1863, William Jr. served in the Civil War; it appears he was wounded in the wrist. Returning to Troy, he studied law under T. Banker, and, like his older brother, Miles, after being admitted to the bar, he became a partner in his father's firm. In Troy he founded the Literary Society and was active on a debate team. By his early twenties, he had appeared in court on several occasions and soon was considered to be his father's equal in the courtroom, an extremely high compliment. To the envy of many, William A. Beach, one of the foremost court room lawyers of his age, could take the greatest pride in his namesake.

In November, 1864, William Jr. married Isabella Ellis, the daughter of a lawyer from Syracuse. The following year, 1865, the young couple had a son.

The younger Beach and his wife decided to spend the summer season of 1866 in Saratoga; the young couple and their child stayed at his grandmother's home on Broadway. William Jr. was born in Saratoga and, before his father's move to Troy, lived in that resort city for his first nine years. By August 25, the season was winding down; coincidentally it was also William Jr.'s twenty-fifth birthday. He decided to spend the morning shooting game birds with one of his childhood friends named Lowery, on a farm west of the city. By nine in the morning they decided that the game was scarce; they decided to cut the hunt short and to return to town. According to reports in the newspapers, on the way into the village, the carriage hit a stone and Beach's gun slid out of the carriage. The gun was cocked and, in a freak accident, the hammer hit the wheel and discharged. The gun, which was only a couple of feet away from William Jr. when it discharged, sent its shot into his right temple. William, who was driving at the time, passed the reins to his friend and ordered that the wagon be rushed into town. Beach knew that he was dying and dictated notes for his wife, father and a friend. By the time they got the carriage back to his grandmother's, three miles away, Beach was failing fast and was already unconscious. They sent for a doctor, but it was too late; William Jr. died before noon.

There is one major inconsistency with this story, as it has been reported. People then drove carriages from the left seat. If Beach were driving, how could the gun have slipped out with the discharge hitting him in the right temple?

The funeral was held from his grandmother's house. So many people wanted to attend that arrangements were made for a special train to get everyone to the service.

Throughout Mrs. Robinson's trial, William A. Beach Sr. was consumed with maintaining his name, and projecting his image of being invincible. That day it was clear that he was no longer unbeatable, and he had lost the child who most notably exhibited own his qualities.

During the trial, **Richard C. Jennyss** was called as a witness for the defense. Jennyss was the young lawyer who visited Mrs. Robinson shortly after she was placed in jail. The real motivation for Jennyss's visits was not the best interests of Mrs. Robinson, but an effort to retrieve letters that Mather had written to her.

Richard C. Jenyss

In 1860, six years after the trial, Jennyss married. He fathered six children, five daughters and a son. The boy was named Richard, after his father. To avoid confusion, Jennyss's son was referred to by his middle name, Louis. Like his father, Louis became a lawyer. Like the sons of other lawyers, he had every opportunity. Through his father's connections, he was trained in the best firms in Troy. Louis was considered to be brilliant, suave and possessed of a sense of determination that would take him to the top of his field. Louis had only two weaknesses, good looks and a mild-mannered personality.

In the late 1880's, Louis took on a divorce case, representing Minnie Moore Nelligan, wife of Thomas Nelligan. Minnie was the rebellious daughter of William Moore. the wealthy mill owner from Cohoes. She was raised amid grace and style, but somehow was able to escape its lure, instead seeking adventure and danger-ous relations. Minnie first rocked the foundation of Cohoes society when she eloped with Thomas, who was well "below her station". Thomas was only an employee of her father. Her marriage to Nelligan was considered unnatu-ral, and she soon became bored. In an unusual gesture, Nelligan was cooperative and granted her a divorce.

Minnie's wild nature was only warming up. Soon after her divorce, she eloped for a second time; this time she married her attorney, Richard Louis Jennyss.

R. Louis Jennyss

Shortly after their marriage, Jennyss realized that Minnie's reputation would not allow them into the social circle to which his family was accustomed. In 1889, the couple relocated to Murphy, North Carolina, a rural logging town. Although her prospects may have been limited, Minnie was able once more to attract a man into her web. The man was a lumber dealer from Ashville named Will Wilkinson. Noticing that the two were together too often, Louis warned both his wife and Wilkinson to "desist" in showing atten-tion to each other.

In early July, 1895, Louis and Wilkinson met by coinci-dence at a train depot. It was 3:00 in the afternoon. During the con-versation that ensued, Wilkinson asked Louis when he was going to return home. After learning that Louis planned to be away overnight, Wilkinson boarded a train bound for Blue Ridge. Six miles down the track, near Louis's home, Wilkinson jumped off the moving train. He then walked to Louis and Minnie's rural house. Wilkinson told Minnie that her husband was not going to return that night. Since Wilkinson had to take the early train to Ashville, the two lovers agreed to spend together what time they could, then she would take him to the station during the night.

At 11:00 p.m. Louis decided to start for home rather than to stay all night. When he neared his house, Louis tied his horse and approached on foot. It was about 2:30 in the morning when Minnie and Wilkinson boarded the family cart and headed for the station. They had started down the lane when they heard a shot; wounded, Minnie slumped forward. With horses startled by the sound of a gun, the cart proceeded down the lane at a high rate of speed. Louis cut across the open field in an attempt to head off the couple when they reached the road to turn toward town. As he approached the road, Louis fired four more shots.

One mile down the road, Wilkinson met a farmer who was driving a buggy. Wilkinson switched carts with the man, telling him to take the better cart and to get a doctor. He then drove Minnie to a farmhouse where he put her on two chairs on a porch and tried to awaken the owners. In the meantime, Louis had returned to his own team and was in pursuit of his wife and Wilkinson. When Louis came to the farmhouse, he found his wife alone, dead, on the porch. Wilkinson drove on to Murphy where he boarded a train to Ashville. When questioned later, Wilkinson would say that he went to Ashville in search of legal advice. The feeling in the community was that Wilkinson was a coward, running away and leaving a wounded woman behind.

Like his father, Louis Jennyss's life was forever changed by the love of a man for a woman. Two years later. Louis Jennyss would be living in California; although his son was still alive, Richard Jennyss, the father, had lost his son just as Henrietta had lost Mather.

Before Mrs. Robinson's trial began, **Anson Bingham** married Laura McClellan. Between 1841 and 1851, they had five children. To demonstrate his true admiration for his wife, the first born was named Laura. The child died before reaching the age of two. The next born was Henry, who died before the age of three. Again as a true testament to his love, Bingham named the third child Laura, after his beloved wife. The youngest Laura died in 1867 at the age of 21. Their fourth child was named Harriet, she lived to be age five. The last was Robert, who lived to twenty-two. Anson had not named any of his children after himself, but he named two of his daughters, after his adored wife. Bingham outlived all five of his children and his beloved wife. He died alone in 1882. What greater tragedy could he have know than to experience the deaths of all the people he loved and to die alone?

***

The trio of Judge Ira Harris, Martin I. Townsend and Henry Hogeboom had the most profound impact on the trial; Townsend for insisting on the pursuit of the insanity defense; Hogeboom for his belief that he, and only he, could know the truth, and Harris for his charge to the jury, which virtually denied insanity as a reasonable defense. The three had put the jury in a position in which the members could not rule on her guilt or innocence, but only on her sanity.

Before examining what happened to the biggest players, Townsend, Hogeboom and Harris, it is interesting to see what effect Mrs. Robinson may have had on the lesser characters in the trial. No records could be found of Mary Dillon. Mrs. Lanagan became known as Mrs. Lanigan; she was still living in the late 1860's with a daughter-in-law who ran a grocery store on River Street in Troy.

Sheriff John Price lost the next election. Among the records of the following years was a notice of his arrest for chicken theft. The man who held Henrietta in jail for the highest offense, found himself in jail for one of the lowest.

And then there were Hogeboom, Harris, and Townsend

Henry Hogeboom tried to live his life in the vein of the truest Victorian virtues. This adherence to values was evident in his church membership, lifestyle and the standards to which he held himself throughout his life. Like so many of the lawyers in the case, Hogeboom was also a man with deep American roots. Unlike most of the other attorneys, his ancestors were Dutch, while those of the others were English. His grandfather and father were the Sheriffs of Columbia County; his grandfather was killed in the line of duty during the Rent Wars. Henry understood and lived the Calvinist doctrine of service to the community.

Hogeboom was raised to be a professional, choosing the law as his vocation. By the time of Mrs. Robinson's trial, Hogeboom had already served as a judge. Above all else, Hogeboom was a family man. In 1832, Hogeboom married Jane Eliza Riverington, the granddaughter of an officer in the Revolutionary War and daughter of a major landholder. Unlike some of his peers, Hogeboom was devoted to his wife. In the late 1870's, in celebration of America's one-hundredth birthday, a rash of local histories were written. In those which included Hogeboom, a large section was devoted to his wife. She was considered to be refined, cultured, charming and very beautiful. Hogeboom's devotion to the sanctity of marriage and to the role of women may have played into the attitude toward Mrs. Robinson and her lifestyle that he exhibited so consistently during the trial.

Like every other lawyer in this trial, Hogeboom, and his wife, had lost the son named for his father. The boy, Henry, was five at the time of his death. They had three other children.

In March of 1858, four years after the trial, Hogeboom's wife, Jane, died at the age of 46. Her death was reported to be the result of "lung inflammation", which probably was Tuberculosis, but may have been pneumonia. She had tried, literally, to pull life-giving air into her lungs until her body did not have the strength to go on. On a personal level, Hogeboom was destroyed by her death. Although a judge, he rarely socialized, never remarried, and his numerous obituaries and records of his life concurred that with her death "all the joy and light of his life" went out. Apparently, he was then "free from all other earthly love except that ... for his and her children." Refusing to remarry was not an easy task for a successful widower; the Civil War was about to begin, and the number of widows in the area was impressive.

Hogeboom and Mrs. Robinson were both devoted to one partner. When her relationship ended, she went into public trying to find peace in the company of others. When Hogeboom's relationship ended, he went into seclusion trying to find peace within himself. The man who professed to sanctify marriage was left without one. The man who had used his words to strangle the future of Mrs. Robinson watched as the one he loved died from lack of air.

Judge Ira Harris, in many ways, suffered the worst of the curse. According to all accounts, Harris had presided over a very fair trial and was able to avoid being visibly provoked when his demands were not met (i.e. the veil). At the same time, in his charge to the jury, Harris had painted the adjudicators into a corner. He told the jurors that the defense had failed to claim that Mrs. Robinson was not guilty. He said that they had only presented a case based on insanity. This was not true; the defense, on numerous occasions, had said that a case against Mrs. Lanagan would better suit the prosecution than the one against Mrs. Robinson.

Harris was an unusual man. He was an intellectual by nature; his personal library consisted of over 3,500 books. It was not so much by choice that Harris became a judge, as it was by accident. He was befriended by Thurlow Weed, the "Little Dictator". In 1860, Weed had thrown his support behind William Seward to be President. When the Republicans nominated Abraham Lincoln, Lincoln knew that he needed the support of New York, so he enlisted Seward to be his Secretary of State. That left open the position of Senator from New York. At that time, Senators were elected by their state legislatures, not by the people at large. There was a fierce fight for the position; Horace Greeley, Weed's sworn enemy, vied for the position. Weed originally was supporting a candidate from New York City (the same man who had prosecuted the case against Mather). In the meantime Harris had decided to accept a position at the newly-formed Albany Law School. As a show of respect, Harris's name, along with five others, was placed in nomination. A group of twenty legislators, who did not want either Greeley or Weed's handpicked nominee, clung to Harris on ballot after ballot. When, after six ballots, it became apparent that Weed's candidate could not pull the necessary majority, Weed abandoned his man. Weed, the manipulator, switched his support to Harris, and, after two more ballots, Harris was elected.

Harris turned out to be a better friend than a legislator. His name was not associated with the introduction of any significant legislation while he was in the Senate. However, soon after he moved to Washington, Harris became one of President Lincoln's closest allies and, even more importantly, the President's personal friend. The Lincolns and the Harrises were so close that, on the evening of April 14, 1865, as the Civil War was winding down, the Lincolns decided to spend a restful evening at Ford's Theater. Mrs. Lincoln asked Senator Harris and his wife to accompany

Clara Harris

them. Harris was not able to attend, but suggested that his daughter, Clara, and her fiancé (and stepbrother) Major Henry Rathbone, would welcome the opportunity to join the First Couple. That night John Wilkes Booth slipped into the President's Box and shot Lincoln. As Booth ran to the side of the box, Rathbone rose to restrain the assassin. Booth had planned for this contingency, carrying a dagger in addition to the pistol. On his way to the rail, Booth stabbed Rathbone in the chest.

Unlike most of those involved with the trial, Harris did not name one of his two sons after himself. For a brief time, it looked as though he might lose a stepson as a result of the stabbing. In true Robinson style, however, Harris would not be fortunate and lose his soon-to-be son-in-law.

Rathbone and Clara Harris married and had three children. Rathbone was a true Republican and, following the election of 1880, President Cleveland named Rathbone as Consul to Germany. At the same time, Rathbone's cousin, the wealthy industrialist from Albany, was the Consul to France. Henry Rathbone turned out to be a very jealous husband; his jealousy was so deep that he even resented the time his wife spent with their children. On the night of December 23, 1883, Rathbone shot and stabbed Clara in their home in Germany. He then attempted suicide. The German court system proved to be more lenient that its American cousin. Rathbone was not convicted of murder; as he was considered to be insane. Rathbone spent the rest of his life in an asylum in Germany.

Harris, who had, through his closing, claimed that Mrs. Robinson was sane, lost his favorite daughter to a man who was insane.

Martin I. Townsend, the man who Mrs. Robinson said had abandoned her at the time of sentencing, had only one child who lived to be an adult. The child was a daughter, Frances, who attended Emma Willard, when it was still called the Seminary. Frances married Henry Nason, one of the leading chemists in the country and a professor at RPI.

In the late 1890's, as a tribute, it was common to honor a person by giving a silver cup as recognition of a lifetime of achievements. When Martin Townsend received his in cup 1899, he remarked that he had not been blessed with any sons, but hoped that the many men whom he had mentored and his grandson would carry on his tradition of hard work and devotion to the community. These comments showed Townsend's lack of respect for women, at least with regard to them for offspring.

Frances and Henry Nason had only one child, a boy named Henry Jr., who literally had everything. His parents were upper middle class. He was raised in a house with three servants; his family had a "name", as exhibited by both his father and maternal grandfather. Naturally brilliant, Henry Jr. went to Williston Academy, a preparatory school. To his parents' delight, he won an academic scholarship to attend Yale University. At Yale, he continued to show his academic gift and was a member of the most scholarly clubs. Immediately after Yale, he went to Columbia Law School. In early summer of 1888, a few months short of his twenty-third birthday, Henry Jr. was already a lawyer and had formed a partnership with his esteemed grandfather, Martin I. Townsend. In 1896, when he was only 31, Henry Nason Jr., became a judge of the New York State Supreme Court. By 1903, Henry Jr. still had not married, but that could be explained by his station in life. To farmers and others who ran small businesses, a child is a future worker and, thus, an asset.

Judge Henry Nason

To a young professional, like Henry Nason Jr., a child was a financial liability, since the child would be expected to attend only the best schools. In the Victorian Era it was common for young professional men to wait until they were well into their thirties, or, as was the case with Richard Jennyss, until their forties to marry. These professional men often married much younger women.

To anyone who might have thought that there was a curse attached to those involved in Mrs. Robinson's trial, the Townsend/Nason family might have appeared to put that thought to rest; a least until the four month period from December, 1902 to April, 1903. First, in December, 1902, came the unexpected death of Florence Townsend Nason; her husband was already deceased. In his nineties when his daughter died, Martin, who was not well, declined rapidly and died in March of 1903. Suddenly, Henry Nason Jr. was a wealthy man with the burden of carrying the family legacy alone. Emotionally, he had not been well for some time. He had taken off the preceding summer to travel and to rest. Now, as spring brought on the promise of summer, he faced the world by himself.

Late in the morning of Monday, March 30, 1903, Henry Jr. stopped at his office in Troy to sign some papers. He visited briefly with his secretary and his clerk. He told them that a classmate from college was in Albany and that the two were going to have dinner together. As he was leaving, the clerk noted that Henry was not wearing an overcoat. Nason responded that, despite the gentle rain, he did not a need coat, and he left. A few hours later, as Henry was leaving a pharmacy in Albany, he ran into a fellow judge. Like his clerk, the judge inquired about Henry's failure to wear a coat, asking whether he was not afraid he might, in the language of the day, "take a cold." Henry remarked, "It might be well if I take cold, for then it would take my mind off the troubles I have had with the loss of my devoted mother and grandfather."

The next morning, Henry did not show up at his office. His law clerk and secretary made inquiries; to their surprise, they learned that the classmate, whom Henry said that he was meeting on the previous evening, had never even planned to come to Albany. The day was spent searching for the young judge among his friends. By Wednesday it was clear that something was amiss. The police were alerted, and a reward of $500 was offered for information leading to his discovery.

On Friday morning, a man who lived south of Kenwood, the great estate of the Rathbone's, Ira Harris's brother-in-law, took out his new hound to continue his training as a hunting dog. As he crossed an open field that led into some of the deepest thicket in Albany County, the man let the dog loose. The dog ran into the brush and started to bark. Thinking the dog had found a rabbit's warren, the man took his time joining the hound. When the man finally reached the dog, he found that it was barking at the discovery of a man's body.

Henry Jr. was found with his face covered in gauze, and three bottles lying nearby. Two of the bottles had pharmaceutical labels indicating that they contained laudanum and chloroform. The third bottle held liquor. His money, watch, and diamond tie pin were still on his person. It was soon determined that after he went to Albany, he used an assumed name to purchase the laudanum at one drugstore. At a second drugstore, the same one a which he encountered the judge who asked about his overcoat, Henry had purchased chloroform. It was legal to purchase chloroform to help someone sleep, if they had a toothache. The bottle which contained the liquor was not opened; it was evident that Henry had taken laudanum to reduce the pain of the chloroform, which can burn the skin. He then had strapped the gauze to his face and poured the chloroform onto the gauze. Without the laudanum, this would have been a very painful death.

Martin I. Townsend, the man who measured the worth of his life through the accomplishments of his grandson, saw that grandson abandon the family legacy through suicide, just as Martin had abandoned Mrs. Robinson almost fifty years before.

***

By 1903, the woman known only as Henrietta Robinson had only two years left to live. Every single person who hurt her during the trial had suffered a personal loss in some violent manner. In VanSantvoord's case, it was himself. Each of the attorneys who named a son after himself, either lost that son by a tragic death or the son caused the tragic death of the one he loved. In the case of Ira Harris, he lost his daughter. Was this bad luck, or "the sins of the father"? That is a question that each reader will have to answer for himself or herself. However, the statistical probability of each person who had been detrimental to Mrs. Robinson suffering such losses is astronomical.

***

John C. Mather was a man in love with money, power and the use of both. To him, the ability to connect to sources, to have people leap when he entered, was the essence of life. After the trial, life in Troy was too embarrassing for Mather. He moved to New York City where he was immediately adopted by the Tammany Hall organization.

In 1856 he was elected to the State Senate by the greatest majority of anyone in the state until that time. His service was controversial. He was chair of the Canal Commission, yet he opposed a levy on rail traffic. He reduced funding for the construction of a new city hall in his adopted city of New York. He claimed to represent all of the people, yet he would take advantage of a deal that helped himself at the expense of others.

In 1860, he was nominated for Congressman from lower Manhattan. By this time he was reporting himself to be almost ten years younger than his real age. As a candidate backed by Tammany Hall, his election was assured. One week before the election, and after the ballots were printed, for reasons never explained, Mather withdrew from the race.

The scandals of his life were not over; Mather was investigated for the purchase of Federal land in Minnesota. The land had previously been a fort, and the purchase price appeared to be well below the fair market value. Once again he beat the charges.

Mather remarried and, in 1876, he and his second wife moved to Watertown, New York. He had some money, but his power was gone. He died in relative obscurity.

There is no record indicating, if those involved with Mrs. Robinson, ever realized the connection of the tragedy in their family, with those in the other families.

End?

Moves for release

By the time Mrs. Robinson had spent fifteen years in prison, a movement had been started to obtain her release. The person or persons behind the movement were never revealed, but in 1870 Rensselaer County District Attorney Banker received a letter from the Governor asking for background information regarding the case of Mrs. Robinson. There were questions asked concerning who was behind the request. The assumption was that there was still someone with "affectionate interest." The Veiled Murderess, who had been lucky enough to be almost forgotten by the world, was suddenly the center of a new debate over the appropriateness of a pardon in a Capital conviction. The *Troy Times* warned that the Governor had a delicate duty. The *Times* questioned the appropriateness of prison versus an insane asylum. In contrast, the *Press* called on the Governor not to let a known murderer free with a pardon, but they felt that confinement to an asylum would be acceptable under the circumstances.

In 1875, a bill passed both houses of the state legislature that allowed any person sentenced to life in prison who had served fifteen years, to be conditionally released, providing that their behavior in prison warranted such consideration. Three women in the state were affected by the new law. By this time, Henrietta Robinson had served twenty years and had been moved from Sing Sing to Auburn prison.

She was considered to be insane and was not released.

Another curse?

In November of 1883, John O'Brien an attorney in Troy and a native of Utica, died. It turned out that O'Brien's career had been many things, none of them were financially rewarding. O'Brien had a tough life. He was born in Ireland in 1820, the illegitimate son of a priest and a lady of "high rank." His mother, who was Protestant, kept his birth a secret, probably saying that he was the child of a servant in the household. He received an excellent education, and, at the age of nineteen, came to America to attend Cazenovia College. He received a monthly allowance of $25, a huge sum at the time. It was his mother's expectation that he could become a

Protestant minister. Lacking an interest in the ministry, he left college and moved to the metropolis of Utica, where he joined the Catholic church. Suddenly, the money stopped, and he learned later that his mother had died.

At the same time, he had been smitten with a young woman from one of the better families in Utica. He wanted to marry her, but she insisted on a marriage in a Protestant church, something this newly-converted Catholic could not accept. For religious reasons, the engagement was broken off, and O'Brien never married.

In the spring of 1853, O'Brien was working late in his office at the corner of Third and Congress in Troy. He looked up from his work and saw a lady dressed in a black silk dress standing in front of him. The woman claimed that she, like he, had been born of noble parents. Her parents had sent her away because of mistakes that she had made in her youth. She said that she wanted to talk to him about his own heritage. The woman left after O'Brien refused to tell her anything.

Three weeks later, the entire community became fixated on a double murder in the upper side of town. Two days after the murder, a police officer came to O'Brien's office. The officer told him that, in searching the "Veiled Murderess's" house, they had found a handkerchief with the initials J. O'B. They wanted to know if the handkerchief was his. O'Brien swore at the time that he had never met the lady and that the handkerchief did not belong to him. Thinking about the situation after the officer left, he remembered that the mysterious woman had come to his office on the same night that his laundry was delivered. He went home, checked his clothes and found that he was missing a handkerchief.

Afraid that a connection between the Veiled Murderess and himself would be discovered, for many years he told the story of the mysteries to no one. With time, his style worked against him, and he lost virtually all of his clients. He loitered around the courthouse in clothes that were outdated; he died a very poor man. The story of the mysterious visitor appeared in his obituary, which ran in many newspapers, including the *National Police Gazette*. He was a lawyer who was suddenly most famous in death for the association with the client that he did not represent.

***

By 1897, Henrietta Robinson had spent forty-four years either in jail or prison. That was, at the very least, one and one half times as long as she had spent as a free person. In November of that year, the story suddenly burst back on the pages of newspapers throughout the country. The issue again was the true identity of Mrs. Robinson. A woman, Mrs. Charlotte Norris, who had attended Emma Willard Seminary and was a classmate of Charlotte Wood, had visited Mrs. Robinson in Sing Sing thirty years before. With this breaking news, the *Press* took a slightly different perspective, saying that, if Mrs. Robinson had not worn the veil, there would have been very little interest in her. Knowing her proven political connections shows that the *Press,* more than forty years after the incident, had lost some to the true dynamics of this case.

After Mrs. Robinson's death, in 1905, Mrs. Norris, the woman who had caused the stir in 1897, was interviewed. The woman had visited Mrs. Robinson for more than an hour while she was at Sing Sing (prior to 1870). She was apparently one of the few people who had been granted a meeting by Mrs. Robinson and prison officials. During their meeting, Mrs. Norris immediately identified Charlotte. Charlotte told her former classmate that she had married Sir William Elliot. In Mrs. Norris's account, Charlotte claims to have left her husband after a couple of years. As soon as Mrs. Norris left the cell, officials of Sing Sing beseeched her to tell them the identity of their prisoner. She refused, honoring a request by Charlotte that her family be spared the disgrace that her life had been.

***

On May 14, 1905, the woman known as Henrietta Robinson died in Mattawan Hospital for the Criminally Insane. She had spent the last fifteen years of her life at Mattawan. She had been a quiet patient, expending most of her time making lace. A year before her death, she told one of the physicians that she was from one of the English titled families. As her health was giving out, and her death was near, the hospital authorities asked if she might like to give out her name to clear the record. She said that she had kept the secret for the fifty years she had been in prison, and it would die with her.

When news of Mrs. Robinson's death reached Troy, *The Record* received a dispatch from Chicago. In the dispatch, Mrs. Norris, from the articles in 1897, reiterated her claim that

Henrietta Robinson had attended Emma Willard as Charlotte Wood. In the eight years between the first account and Mrs. Robinson's death, Mrs. Norris had visited her in jail one more time. Over the years, Mrs. Robinson had aged in that hard way brought about by a life without the benefit of light and social companionship. Mrs. Robinson sat in a rocking chair, within her room, making lace. She was dressed in a simple black cotton dress which was complimented by a large lace collar and matching lace cuffs. The inmate had made both; in fact, her only interest by this time was the making of lace.

The 1905 article added much more detail to the account of the earlier visit by Mrs. Norris. She said that she went to the prison and asked the female warden for permission to meet with Mrs. Robinson, saying that she had an idea as to who she really was. The warden summoned a guard go to get Mrs. Robinson. "In a few moments I saw a stately woman, just past middle age, come down the iron stairs with a matron." Mrs. Norris said that she and the prisoner immediately recognized each other. The prisoner calling Mrs. Norris by her maiden name. After the two embraced in the style of the day, the woman whispered into Mrs. Norris's ear, "Don't mention my name, I implore you." During their time alone, Mrs. Norris learned that Charlotte's brother had visited soon after her arrest. On that visit he had "extracted the promise that she would never disgrace the family by revealing her name."

Mrs. Norris said that all of the Wood sisters were attractive. That one of the other sisters, while a student at the Seminary, had fallen madly in love with John C. Mather. When Charlotte was banished from her father's house, she had returned to Troy where she met Mather. The two became romantically and physically involved. It was through his considerable influence that her brother had been able to pull off the scam at the reunion. At the end of the interview, Mrs. Robinson, who was not under the influence of any drugs, claimed that she and Mather had been married in a hotel with the proprietor as the witness.

There was yet one more account to be dealt with. When Mrs. Robinson died, the American newspapers carried the various stories relating the crime and the matter of her identity. It was inevitable that the Canadian newspapers would discover the accounts. *The Montreal Daily Witness* printed a letter from a Mr. Francis Davis who claimed to be a cousin of the Wood family. His letter, which is not easy to follow, said that Charlotte Wood married William Elliott. Lady Elliot had a laundress whose daughter had a "likeness to Miss Charlotte Wood [that] was most remarkable." Davis made many claims, some of which are truly incorrect, including one that Mrs. Robinson had killed her own husband and that Lady Elliott used her influence to spare the imposter the death penalty. Davis also said that one of Charlotte's brothers had also married into the Elliott family.

Over the years, Mrs. Henrietta Robinson had been given many, widely divergent, birthrights. She was said to have been born to a wealthy family in Canada; it was said that she was the illegitimate daughter of one of the sons of the same family. There were reports that she was a neighbor of the same Canadian family who used an endowment to open a tavern. It was also claimed that she was the daughter of a laundress who worked for a member of the family in England. She was even said to have no relationship, but merely looked like the family and used this to gain influence. Perhaps someday, through the use of DNA evidence, the truth will be known, but, for now, we know that she was a woman whose only proven offense was a bad selection of men.

After Mrs. Henrietta Robinson died, prison officials found a small locket sewn into her needle case. When the locket was opened, they found a picture, and a small piece of paper with the following poem written on it:

When first I saw this world of joy and pain,
Assailed by doubt that ever will remain,
I wondered what it meant to live to die –
The question oft I pondered, but in vain.

Index